PRESSURE
GROUPS

access to politics

PRESSURE GROUPS

David Simpson

Series Editor: David Simpson

Hodder & Stoughton

A MEMBER OF THE HODDER HEADLINE GROUP

ACKNOWLEDGEMENTS

The publishers would like to thank the following for permission to reproduce copyright photographs:

The Hutton Getty Collection, p.20; Priestley, *The Independent*, p.36; NALGO and John Twinning, p.68; National Trust Photographic Library and John Garrett, p.91

The publishers would like to thank *Talking Politics*, the Journal of the Politics Association for permission to reproduce copyright material.

Orders: please contact Bookpoint Ltd, 39 Milton Park, Abingdon, Oxon OX14 4TD. Telephone: (44) 01235 400414, Fax: (44) 01235 400454. Lines are open from 9.00–6.00, Monday to Saturday, with a 24 hour message answering service. Email address: orders@bookpoint.co.uk

A catalogue record for this title is available from The British Library

ISBN 0 340 747587

First published 1999
Impression number 10   9   8   7   6   5   4   3   2   1
Year   2005   2004   2003   2002   2001   2000   1999

Cover photo from Greenpeace UK

Typeset by Transet Limited, Coventry, England.
Printed in Great Britain for Hodder & Stoughton Educational, a division of Hodder Headline plc, 338 Euston Road, London NW1 3BH by Redwood Books, Trowbridge, Wilts.

CONTENTS

PREFACE

A/AS Level syllabuses in Government and Politics aim to develop knowledge and understanding of the political system of Britain. They cover its local, national and European Union dimensions, and include comparative studies of aspects of other political systems, in order to ensure an understanding of the distinctive nature of the British political system. The minimum requirements for comparative study are aspects of systems with a separation of powers, how other systems protect the rights of individuals and how other electoral systems work.

Access to Politics is a series of concise topic books which cover the syllabus requirements, providing students with the necessary resources to complete the course successfully.

General advice on approaching exam questions

To achieve high grades you need to demonstrate consistency. Clearly address all parts of a question, make good use of essay plans or notes, and plan your time to cover all the questions.

Make your answers stand out from the crowd by using contemporary material to illustrate them. You should read a quality newspaper and listen to or watch appropriate programmes on radio and television.

Skills Advice

You should comprehend, synthesise and interpret political information in a variety of forms:

- Analyse and evaluate political institutions, processes and behaviour, political arguments and explanations.
- Identify parallels, connections, similarities and differences between aspects of the political systems studied.
- Select and organise relevant material to construct arguments and explanations leading to reasoned conclusions.
- Communicate the arguments with relevance, clarity and coherence, using vocabulary appropriate to the study of Government and Politics.

David Simpson

1

INTRODUCTION

THIS BOOK LOOKS at the role of pressure groups in the British political system and their relationships with other institutions. It includes a discussion of such concepts as pluralism and corporatism.

SUMMARY OF PERSPECTIVES

Early studies of pressure groups in the British political system were dominated by the decision-making methodology, concentrating upon decisions taken by government and attempting to isolate the influence of pressure groups upon such decisions. Examples of this micro-level approach were the case studies of the British Medical Association (Eckstein, 1960) and the National Farmers Union (Self and Storing, 1962) in the 1960s.

The decision-making methodology has been criticised from an **elitist**, or sometimes a **Marxist**, perspective. The most fundamental criticism originated from Marxist structuralists such as Poulantzas. He believed that the nature of the relationship between the State and the ruling class is determined by the nature of capitalism as an economic system. The State, or in its most obvious manifestation the government, is in a fundamental sense the agent of the ruling class. This means that to study ongoing decisions is largely irrelevant. What is crucial is the nature of the relationship between the classes in any given capitalist society. To Poulantzas, behavioural evidence associated with a decision-making analysis would be irrelevant or, at best, of peripheral importance. However, increasingly Marxists have talked about the relative autonomy of the State. The most common view is that while the State serves the interests of the owners and controllers of the means of production in the long run, it has autonomy in the operation of both the economic and the political systems.

A less fundamental criticism of the decision-making methodology is that which was first associated with Bachrach and Baratz (1962). They argued that there are two faces of power. Decision-making analysis by its very nature concentrates upon decisions actually taken, called by Bachrach and Baratz 'concrete decisions'. 'Of course power is exercised when A participates in the making of decisions that affect B', they wrote. However, power is also exercised when A devotes his or her energies

> *to creating or reinforcing social and political values and institutional practices that limit the scope of the political process to the public consideration of only those issues which are comparatively innocuous to A. To the extent that A succeeds in doing this, B is prevented, for all practical purposes, from bringing to the fore any issues that might in their resolution be seriously detrimental to A's set of preferences.*

In other words, a group or individuals can also have influence by preventing concrete decisions being taken, or by controlling the 'parameters of decision-making'.

Steven Lukes extended the analysis of Bachrach and Baratz by identifying three faces of power, namely first, the capacity to influence ongoing concrete decisions; second, the capacity to stop certain suggested decisions being considered within the political arena; and third, the capacity to shape the political values of the situations or institutions within which decisions are taken, so that certain alternative policies are not even suggested, let alone considered.

This methodological criticism is associated with an elitist critique of **pluralism** (for pluralism as a concept analysing the role of pressure groups in the political system, see Chapter 3, and for elitism as a criticism of that analysis, see Chapter 6).

The focus of pressure-group studies changed in the 1970s to a macro-level approach with the concept of **corporatism** (see Chapter 3).

More recently, the academic debate has moved on to a *meso-level* approach (midway, that is, between the micro- and macro-level approaches) with the concept of **policy networks** (see again Chapter 3). Examples of this approach include Smith on the agricultural policy community.

The empirical study of pressure groups shifted to the **European Union** after the adoption of the internal market (see Chapter 4).

There has also been an increasing emphasis on the role of single-issue pressure groups (Grant, 1996). Some of them are referred to as **'new social movements'** which emphasise a lack of hierarchy and formal organisation. The classic example in Britain has been the animal-rights movement and, in particular, the protest at ports over the export of live calves (see Appendix 3). However, Brent Spar also focused attention on the role of Greenpeace as an environmental pressure group 'able to transfer decision-making about decommissioning from the British policy community to the more open international issue network' (Bennie, 1998).

2

THE ROLE OF PRESSURE GROUPS

Introduction

THIS CHAPTER WILL distinguish between pressure groups and political parties, define a pressure group, and explain the increased importance of pressure groups.

It will distinguish between 'sectional' groups and 'cause' groups, and explain the growth of cause groups.

Finally, it will distinguish between 'insider' groups and 'outsider' groups.

Key Points
- The distinction between pressure groups and political parties.
- The definition of a pressure group.
- The increased importance of pressure groups.
- Types of pressure group: sectional groups and cause groups; the growth of cause groups; insider groups and outsider groups.

PRESSURE GROUPS AND POLITICAL PARTIES

Seyd and Whiteley (1992) suggest five reasons why political parties are considered essential to democracy:

1 They aggregate the mass of interests in society, without which politics would be dominated by special interests.
2 They recruit and socialise future political leaders.
3 Party members play an important role in communication between leaders and voters.

4 They contribute to policy-making, ensuring that new ideas get onto the political agenda.
5 They mobilise the vote during election campaigns.

Pressure groups carry out the second, third and fourth functions, but not generally the first and fifth.

Whereas political parties, aggregating the mass of interests in society, are generally concerned with a wide range of public policies, pressure groups, representing special interests, are usually concerned with a small range of public policy. For example, the Pro-Life Alliance was founded in 1996 to oppose abortion, euthanasia and the destruction of human embryos. However, in practice this distinction is not so clear. Some pressure groups, for example the Trades Union Congress (TUC) and the Confederation of British Industry (CBI), take an interest in a wide range of policies.

Some pressure groups mobilise the vote during election campaigns on behalf of candidates supporting their interests. For example, 'constituency plan agreements' between trade unions and selected constituency Labour parties involve some union money-funding constituency election campaigns, in return for which the trade unions have some representation on the general committees of the constituency Labour parties (see p. 67). Other pressure groups mobilise the vote during election campaigns on behalf of their own candidates. For example, the Pro-Life Alliance put up 53 candidates in the General Election of 1997.

Nevertheless, pressure groups mobilise the vote during election campaigns as part of a strategy to influence government without themselves seeking to govern. They may put up candidates to draw attention to the level of public concern on a particular issue. For example, the Pro-Life Alliance was more concerned with opposing abortion than with winning seats. Its main national publicity was gained with its plans to trace the development of a foetus, culminating in a very late abortion, in its broadcast. BBC and ITV officials who previewed the tape and were shocked by this sequence ruled that it broke their guidelines on taste and decency. The broadcast was transmitted with the offending material replaced by a caption maintaining that if abortion was indeed too extreme to broadcast, it was too extreme to be legal (Butler and Kavanagh, 1997).

Pressure groups may also put up candidates to draw sufficient votes away from parties to make them lose seats and think again about some aspect of their policies. For example, the Referendum Party was founded in 1995 with the aim of putting up candidates in every seat except where someone was standing who was explicitly committed to a referendum on Britain's future in the European Union (EU), promising to dissolve as soon as the referendum took place. It was therefore not a party as such but a pressure group adopting a particular tactic more generally associated with a political party. Unlike Ross Perot's United We Stand/Reform Party in the USA, the Referendum Party was not seeking to govern the country.

However, pressure groups have on occasions been accused of seeking to govern. For example, trade unions were criticised during the 1970s for undermining the powers of elected governments. Industrial action by the National Union of Mineworkers (NUM) in the winter of 1973–74 led Conservative Prime Minister Ted Heath to call a general election in February 1974 asking the question 'Who Governs?' He lost. Meanwhile, the Trade Union Labour Party Liaison Committee, formed in 1972, was the structural manifestation of a significantly changed relationship between the TUC and the Labour Party. It was composed of six representatives each from the General Council of the TUC, the National Executive Committee of the Labour Party and the Parliamentary Labour Party. The Liaison Committee was crucially involved in the development of the Social Contract. It was through this Committee that the General Council of the TUC exercised influence on the Labour Party's manifestos for General Elections in February and October 1974 (see Appendix 1).

The difficulty of distinguishing clearly between pressure groups and political parties is exacerbated by the fact that pressure groups exist within political parties. For example, the Conservative Group for Europe is a pro-European-involvement pressure group within the Conservative Party; and the Labour Campaign for Electoral Reform is a pressure group within the Labour Party.

THE DEFINITION OF A PRESSURE GROUP

A pressure group may therefore be defined narrowly as an organisation which seeks to influence a comparatively small range of public policy without itself seeking to govern.

Such a narrow definition raises problems. For example, should governmental bodies be regarded as pressure groups? A government department has a 'departmental view' developed over time which seeks to influence a comparatively small range of public policy. However, it has to aggregate the special interests of different pressure groups. For example, the Ministry of Agriculture, Fisheries and Food has to reconcile agricultural, fishing and food interests. A government department also has to place its view within the context of the policy of the government as a whole.

Quasi-autonomous neo-governmental organisations (quangos) pose greater problems. In practice, some act as pressure groups. For example, the Commission for Racial Equality seeks to eliminate racial discrimination and promote equality of opportunity between persons of different racial groups.

Group theorists such as Bentley (1908) define pressure groups in the broad sense that almost any form of organisation that clarifies its objectives in relation to policy and uses its political resources in an attempt to shape public policy is, in effect, a pressure group. What matters is not the constitution of a particular organisation, nor its place within the political system, but its role in relation to the policy-making process. According to Bentley, the process of government must be studied as 'wholly a group process'.

THE INCREASED IMPORTANCE OF PRESSURE GROUPS

Pressure groups have been an important feature of the British political system for over two centuries; for example, the Committee for Effecting the Abolition of the Slave Trade was formed in 1787. However, their relative importance has increased in recent years. As membership of political parties has declined, membership of pressure groups has increased. Far more citizens are now members of pressure groups than of political parties.

In 1997, the three main parties had between them fewer than one million members, compared with more than two million in 1964. Party membership is in decline not only in Britain. It is also declining, for example, in Scandinavia. Only Austria and Germany have seen increases. However, membership of a party in Austria has often been a prerequisite for gaining a council house, and jobs in Germany are often dependent on membership (*Guardian*, 'Analysis party membership', 23 June 1998). In the USA in the 1980s, Cigler and Loomis (1986) noted 'the continuing decline of political parties' abilities to perform key electoral and policy-related activities'.

The over four and a half million membership of environmental pressure groups alone in Britain (see Table 1) is much larger than that of the political parties. This is relatively small compared, for example, with Denmark which has more members of environmental pressure groups than it has total population, because of dual membership (Brenton, 1994). Cigler and Loomis in their 1991 edition noted that in the USA 'large numbers of citizens have become active in an ever increasing number of protest groups, citizens' organisations, and special interest groups.'

Membership of political parties and pressure groups is not, of course, an either/or choice. For example, 16 per cent of Labour Party members surveyed by Seyd and Whitely (1992) were also members of Greenpeace, 8.2 per cent were members of Friends of the Earth (FoE), and 6.8 per cent were members of Amnesty International. Even so, it is clear that many citizens feel more comfortable as members of a pressure group than of a political party. Seyd and Whitely note that many of the individuals who join pressure groups find traditional party organisational structures unattractive.

The rise of a Conservative dominant-party system between 1979 and 1997 (see Simpson, 1998, part of the Access to Politics series), and the landslide parliamentary majority of the Labour Party in 1997, have had two important implications for pressure groups:

	THOUSANDS			
	1971	1981	1989	1995
National Trust	280	1050	2100	2300
Wildlife Trust[1]	64	140	250	260
Royal Society for Protection of Birds	100	440	850	890
World Wide Fund for Nature	12	60	200	210
Woodland Trust	–	20	150	150[2]
Greenpeace	–	30	320	410[2]
Friends of the Earth	1	18	120	230[2]
Council for the Protection of Rural England	21	29	45	45
Ramblers Association	22	37	87	94[2]

Table 1: *Growth in members/financial supporters of leading British environmental groups since 1970*

[1] Formerly Royal Society for Nature Conservation.
[2] 1993 figures.

SOURCE: TOKE, 1996, P. 108.

1 They have increased the importance of pressure groups as a mechanism for questioning and opposing government policy.
2 Party factionalism has given them a new set of targets in the form of dissident party groups at which they can direct their activities (Grant, 1993).

TYPES OF PRESSURE GROUP

SECTIONAL AND CAUSE GROUPS

The traditional distinction between types of pressure group has been between what Stewart (1958) calls 'sectional' groups and 'cause' groups. **Sectional groups** represent a certain section of the community. Their function is to look after the common interests of that section, and their membership is normally restricted to that section. For example, the TUC represents workers in trade unions affiliated to it, and the CBI represents business. **Cause groups** represent some belief or principle. They seek to act in the interests of that cause. Theoretically, their membership is not restricted at all. Anyone can join, and by doing so signify his or her acceptance of the belief or principle. For example, environmental pressure groups such as Greenpeace seek to act in the interests of the environment.

Potter (1961) similarly distinguishes between those pressure groups organising sectional interests and those organising shared attitudes. Groups organising sectional interests purport to speak for their sections in 'defence' of their interests, and groups organising shared attitudes seek to 'promote' the causes arising from the attitudes of their members. The basic function of the former as organisations is to be 'representative', so that they may speak for their sections with authority, and the basic function of the latter is to command forces and resources, so that they may use them to further their cause. Potter uses the terms 'spokesman' groups and 'promotional' groups to distinguish between these two types of pressure group.

Sectional groups have been referred to as interest groups, but this can be confusing as sometimes the term interest group has been used to refer to pressure groups in general.

The distinction between sectional and cause groups is blurred by the existence of pressure groups which are, on the face of it, sectional but which represent some belief or principle, seeking to act in the interest of a cause. For example, the British Dental Association is a sectional group looking after the common interests of dentists, but seeks to act in the interests of a cause when supporting water fluoridation. Sectional groups sometimes establish groups to act in the interests of a cause. For example, the Royal College of Physicians set up Action on Smoking and Health (ASH) in 1971 to campaign against smoking.

The growth of cause groups

Cause groups have grown in numbers, particularly environmental ones. For example, FoE increased its membership from 1,000 in 1971 to 230,000 in 1993; the Royal Society for the Protection of Birds (RSPB) from nearly 100,000 in 1971 to 890,000 in 1995; Greenpeace from 30,000 in 1981 to 410,000 in 1993 (see Table 1 on p. 7).

Explanations of the growth of cause groups

Social

Inglehart's (1995) theory of post-material value change utilises Maslow's 'theory of human motivation'. According to Maslow's theory, individuals have a 'hierarchy of needs' ranging from 'physiological' and 'safety' needs to 'esteem' and 'self-actualization' needs. Maslow argues that the clear emergence of 'self-actualization' needs 'rests upon prior satisfaction of the physiological, safety, love and esteem needs'. Inglehart maintains that 'self-realisation' is related to post-materialism and that the possession of post-material values has an actual causal effect on behaviour. With regard to political participation, Inglehart translates these needs into two fundamental categories, material and post-material. The value-change argument maintains that as a growing proportion of the public begins to emphasise post-material values, the composition of the political agenda shifts from traditional economic and security concerns to the non-economic and quality-of-life values of a post-industrial society.

Political
A survey of Amnesty International members, for example, found that 33.5 per cent of male and 42.2 per cent of female members said that one reason for joining the organisation was its non-party political approach (Jordan and Maloney).

Marketing
Jordan and Maloney's (1997) explanation is based on a group perspective, moving the focus from the demand side to the supply side. The efficacy and nature of supply is an important dynamic in the joining decision. Groups can by their marketing strategies alter the level of demand for membership, and given the low monetary costs of subscription to most cause groups, joining/supporting decisions are below a 'threshold of (economic) rationality', that is below the 'cost' of exhaustive analysis.

Jordan and Maloney argue that cause groups attempt to develop membership by using professional marketing strategies which aim both to lower the perception of the economic cost of membership, and to crystallise the predisposed members' concerns. Cause groups offer a mixture of organisational and psychological strategies which help place the joining decision on individuals' agendas.

Modern, large-scale cause groups are the product of mail-order marketing. They are essentially protest businesses. These 'successful' protest businesses would not spend so much time, effort and financial resources to encourage greater mobilisation, and to keep members in once they have crossed the threshold, were it not 'profitable' to do so.

Insider and outsider groups

The distinction between sectional groups and cause groups can be misleading if it is assumed that sectional groups are necessarily more influential than cause groups. There are less influential sectional groups, for example those representing pensioners. On the other hand, a cause group like the RSPB had, by 1992, an annual income of £28 million, far higher than that of the CBI.

Another way of classifying pressure groups is in terms of their relationship to central decision-makers. Grant (1995a) distinguishes between 'insider' groups and 'outsider' groups. **Insider groups**, regarded as legitimate by government, are consulted on a regular basis. **Outsider groups** either do not wish to become involved in regular discussions with officials, or would like to gain recognition by government but are unable to do so.

There is some overlap with the distinction between sectional and cause groups. Most sectional groups are insider groups. However, many cause groups are also insider groups, for example the Council for the Protection of Rural England (CPRE).

Grant's general distinction is further divided into six basic categories. Insider groups are subdivided into three categories:

1 *prisoner groups* which find it particularly difficult to break away from an insider relationship with government either because they are dependent on government for assistance of various kinds, for example the loan of staff or the provision of office accommodation, or because they represent parts of the public sector. English Heritage, a government-appointed body, is an example of a prisoner group.

2 *low-profile* insider groups working largely behind the scenes. For example, the CBI was traditionally a low-profile group which concentrated on reaching 'informed opinion' through publications such as *The Times*.

3 *high-profile* insider groups who cultivate public opinion to reinforce their discussions with government. For example, the CBI has shifted in recent years to a high-profile strategy which has attempted to reach the ordinary person in the street through mass-circulation newspapers and television.

Outsider groups are subdivided into three categories:

1 *potential insider groups*, a transitional category denoting outsider groups which seem to have the capacity to win insider status. They would like to become insider groups but face the problem of gaining government's attention as a prelude to their being accepted as groups which should be consulted in relation to particular policy areas.

2 *outsider groups by necessity* who lack political sophistication in the sense of an understanding of the way in which the political system works and the importance of gaining access to civil servants. They are less endowed with political knowledge and skills. For example, the evidence of the National Association of Ratepayer Action Groups to the Layfield Committee on Local Government Finance, 1976, contained demands which were politically and constitutionally impossible, such as that Parliament should bind itself to vote on rates with the whips off.

3 *ideological outsider groups* who reject the existing political system because they do not think that meaningful change can be achieved through it. For example, Earth First! uses forms of direct action.

Grant's distinction between insider and outsider groups has been criticised by Whitely and Winyard (1987) because it confuses 'the two separate dimensions of strategy and status'. For example, some groups can 'enjoy close contacts with Whitehall yet at the same time make considerable use of the media and public strategies of protest; they are insiders in terms of status, but outsiders in terms of strategy.'

Whitely and Winyard distinguish between *focused* strategies that concentrate the bulk of attention on influencing Whitehall, and *open* strategies that include use of the media. For example, the RSPB, an 'accepted' group in status, used an 'open' strategy to good effect in securing changes to increase the powers of the Environment Agency in-between the publication of the first draft of the Environment Bill and its presentation to the House of Commons in December 1994.

Maloney, Jordan and McLaughlin (1992) distinguish between *insider, outsider* and *threshold* strategies, the latter derived from May and Nugent (1982) who define thresholder groups as 'characterised by strategic ambiguity and oscillation between insider and outsider strategies'. A trade union is an example of a thresholder group.

In terms of status, Maloney, Jordan and McLaughlin distinguish between *core, niche* and *peripheral* insider groups. The distinction between core and niche insider groups is essentially in terms of their range of concern and the number of issues on which they are consulted. The National Farmers Union (NFU) is an example of a core insider group, and the British Poultry Meat Federation an example of a niche insider group. Browne (1990) suggests that

> *the large number of interests in the agriculture domain give rise primarily to very narrow and intensely directed issues … . Policy interest is characterised by obsessive focus on a single facet of agriculture production and food delivery.*

However, Brown uses US data, and agricultural politics in the USA has been centred around particular commodities more than it has in Britain where there has been more aggregation of interests. The real issue, as Jordan, Maloney and McLaughlin see it, concerns the distinction between peripheral insider groups and core or niche insider groups. Peripheral groups are seen as marginal and relatively uninfluential participants in the policy-making process.

SUMMARY

Pressure groups can be distinguished from political parties in that they are usually concerned with a small range of public policy, and they do not seek to govern. A pressure group can thus be defined as an organisation which seeks to influence a comparatively small range of public policy without itself seeking to govern. The relative importance of pressure groups has increased in recent years because of a decline in political party membership and the emergence of a Conservative dominant party system (1979–97) followed by the landslide parliamentary majority of the Labour Party in 1997.

The traditional distinction between types of pressure group has been between sectional groups, looking after the common interests of a section of the community, and cause groups, seeking to act in the interest of a cause. The growth of cause groups may be explained by social, political and marketing factors.

An alternative distinction is that between insider groups, regarded as legitimate by government and consulted on a regular basis, and outside groups, which either do not wish to become involved in regular discussions with officials, or would like to gain recognition by officials but are unable to do so.

STUDY GUIDES

Revision Hints

Make sure you can distinguish between pressure groups and political parties, and can define a pressure group. You should be able to explain the increased importance of pressure groups.

Know the distinction between sectional groups and cause groups, and explanations of the growth of cause groups.

You should also be able to distinguish between insider groups and outsider groups.

Exam Hints

Answering short questions on 'The Role of Pressure Groups'

1 a Distinguish between pressure groups and political parties.
   b Why is it sometimes difficult to distinguish clearly between the two?

You should be able to produce two distinctions between pressure groups and political parties. Demonstrate why it is sometimes difficult to distinguish clearly between the two, providing appropriate examples. Present complex arguments in support of the difficulties in making clear distinctions, for example recognising that pressure groups exist within political parties.

Answering essay questions on 'The Role of Pressure Groups'

2 Discuss the relative importance of pressure groups and political parties.

Do not see this question as an opportunity to write down everything you know about pressure groups and political parties. Mention the decline of political parties in terms of membership, and the increasing membership of pressure groups. A more sophisticated analysis would add the rise of a dominant party system between 1979 and 1997, and the landslide parliamentary majority of the Labour Party in 1997.

Practice Questions

1 a Distinguish between *two* types of pressure group.
   b Explain, with examples, how this distinction is sometimes blurred.
2 Explain the growth of cause groups.

3

PRESSURE GROUPS IN THE POLITICAL SYSTEM

Introduction

THIS CHAPTER WILL define the concepts of pluralism and corporatism. It will explain the rise of corporatism in Britain, the New Right perspective and the fall of corporatism. Finally, it will define the concept of policy networks.

Key Points

- Definitions of the concepts of pluralism and corporatism.
- The rise of corporatism in Britain.
- The New Right and the fall of corporatism.
- The decline of the trade unions.
- Definition of the concept of policy networks.

PLURALISM AND CORPORATISM

The traditional concept used to analyse the role of pressure groups in the political system is pluralism. Here, society is viewed as consisting of a large number of pressure groups, representing all the significant, different interests of the population, who compete with one another for influence over government. This competition operates within the bounds of a consensus about the basic nature of the economic and political system, and about the levels of conflict acceptable. The competition between pressure groups ensures that no one group dominates and that the balance between interests is preserved.

This notion of balance is crucial. Truman (1951) introduces two elements in his conception of the political process, designed to show that there are inherent checks in society which prevent an excessive concentration of power in any one group or set of groups. These elements are overlapping membership and potential pressure groups:

1 Individuals, whose activities are diverse, are bound to be involved in a variety of pressure groups. Members of any one group will be subject to competing interests. For example, members of a Parent–Teacher Association (PTA) assess proposals in the light of the fact that some members will also belong to the Catholic Church, others to the local chamber of commerce, and others to the local taxpayers' pressure group. Thus it is the competing claims of other groups within a given pressure group that force it to reconcile its claims with those of other groups active on the political scene.

2 Any mutual interest or shared attitude is a potential group. New organised pressure groups will be formed as a result of a disturbance in established relationships and expectations anywhere in society. For example, Grant and Marsh (1977) discovered that members of the CBI thought that a principal reason for its existence was the need in society to provide a counterweight to the TUC, a consideration mentioned by almost every director they interviewed. Even though the formation of an organised group may be, for various reasons, extremely difficult, 'it may be this possibility of organisation that alone gives the potential group a minimum of influence in the political process.'

It is also crucial in the concept of pluralism that the government act as an independent arbiter between pressure groups, taking into account both the representations of the groups and the national interest.

Schmitter (1974) distinguishes between pluralism and corporatism. He defines pluralism as a system of pressure-group representation

> *in which the constituent units are organised into an unspecified number of multiple, voluntary, competitive, non-hierarchically ordered and self determined (as to type or scope of interest) categories which are not specially licensed, recognised, subsidised, created or otherwise controlled in leadership selection or interest articulation by the state and which do not exercise a monopoly of representational activity within their respective categories.*

The crucial elements of a pluralist system are thus as follows:

- There are many pressure groups competing with one another for influence over policy.
- The leadership of pressure groups is responsive to its membership.
- While pressure groups may make continuing representations to government, and while such representations may even become institutionalised, the government remains independent of the pressure groups.

- The State, or more accurately the government, is assigned a largely passive role, merely authoritatively allocating scarce resources, with its decisions reflecting the balance between the pressure groups within society at a given time.

Schmitter defines corporatism as a system of pressure-group representation

---

in which the constituent units are organised into a limited number of singular, compulsory, non-competitive, hierarchically ordered and functionally differentiated categories, recognised or licensed (if not created) by the state and granted a deliberate representational monopoly within their respective categories in exchange for observing certain controls on their selection of leaders and articulation of demands and supports.

It differs from pluralism in a number of ways:

- The emphasis is on a limited number of pressure groups representing the major corporations. One might identify key corporations in various areas, but most authors concentrate on the economic and industrial policy fields, and almost exclusively on the pressure groups representing capital and labour. They do so because of the origins of corporatism as an alternative to both Marxism and capitalism, emphasising cooperation between classes rather than conflict or exploitation.
- The pressure groups are hierarchically structured, with group leaders able to 'deliver' their membership.
- In a full corporatist system, the links among the corporations and between the corporations and government would be very close. This unity would result from, and in turn reinforce, a basic consensus about how the political and economic system should operate.
- The 'State', not the 'government', has an active role, although the exact nature of the role depends on the variant of corporatism being considered.

Schmitter distinguishes between what he terms *state corporatism* and *societal corporatism*. Under state corporatism, the State directs the corporations, which are subordinate to and dependent on the State. Under societal corporatism, the corporations are autonomous but cooperate with the State and each other because they recognise that they are mutually interdependent. Lehmbruch (1974) similarly distinguishes between *liberal corporatism* and *authoritarian corporatism*. He argues that the essential features of liberal corporatism are 'the large measure of constitutional autonomy of the groups involved; hence the voluntary character of institutionalized integration of conflicting groups' and 'a high degree of cooperation among these groups themselves in the shaping of public policy'. *Tripartism* is a sub-type of liberal corporatism. In a liberal-corporatist state, the emphasis would be on the relationships between government and a wide range of functional groups, or at least between government and all organisations that represent capital and labour. In contrast, the notion of tripartism emphasises the relationship between government and the peak organisations (that is the major organisations representing capital and labour) only.

THE RISE OF CORPORATISM IN BRITAIN

Britain moved towards a limited form of corporatism, or more accurately a weak version of liberal corporatism, under Conservative and Labour governments from the early 1960s until the end of the 1970s. It was a response to increasing concern about Britain's relative economic decline. Incomes policy, and to a lesser extent prices policy, became central to government economic strategy. This led to an emphasis on the development of effective bargaining relationships with trade unions and employers.

The National Economic Development Council (NEDC), or 'Neddy' as it was called, was set up in 1962 to seek agreement on ways of improving economic performance. It consisted of leading Cabinet ministers, senior civil servants, and representatives of the two sides of industry, the CBI and the TUC each having six representatives. In addition, there were over 20 councils, or 'little Neddies', for particular sectors of industry, again with representatives of employers and trade unions.

THE NEW RIGHT

Olson's (1965) analysis of collective action provides the basis for the New Right view of pressure groups. Olson argues that the individual member of the typical large organisation is in a position where his or her own efforts will not have a noticeable effect on the situation of the organisation, but that the individual can enjoy any improvements made by others whether or not he or she has worked in support of the organisation.

He explains that some large groups are organised by what he calls the 'by-product' theory of large pressure groups. The large economic groups are in fact the by-products of organisations that obtain their strength and support because they perform some function in addition to lobbying for collective goods.

They have the capacity to mobilise a latent group with 'selective incentives'. The only pressure groups that have the 'selective incentives' available are those that either have the authority and capacity to be coercive, or have a source of positive inducements that they can offer the individuals in a latent group.

If, because of some other function it performs, a pressure group has a justification for having a compulsory membership, or if, through this other function, it has obtained the power needed to make membership in it compulsory, that pressure group may then be able to get the resources needed.

In addition to the large pressure groups that depend on coercion, there are those that provide non-collective or private benefits which can be offered to any potential supporter.

Brittan (1975) suggests that 'the pursuit of group self-interest through coercive means in the market place' is a serious threat to democracy. The most obvious form of this is the conflict of different groups of trade unionists – ostensibly with the government or employers, but in reality with each other – for shares of the national product. This rivalry induces more and more sections of the population, including those who have previously relied on individualist efforts, into militant trade-unionist attitudes in self-defence.

THE FALL OF CORPORATISM

The drawback with corporatism in Britain, as distinct from countries such as Sweden, was that both the TUC and the CBI had difficulty in ensuring that their members adhered to agreements reached with government.

For example, the Manpower Services Commission (MSC), set up in 1974 to supervise the operation of the job placement and training services hitherto run by the Department of Employment, was one of the main tripartite agencies. Of the Commission's ten members, three were nominated by the CBI, three were drawn from the trade-union movement, two were appointed after consultations with local authority associations, and one after consultations with professional and educational interests. Thus, the majority of the Commission's membership was drawn from the two main groups representing producers. In the course of its history, the MSC found it increasingly difficult to achieve a consensus that required the corporatist partners to deliver their memberships, for example for trade unions to accept a reduction in youth wages and a radical restructuring of apprenticeships, and for employers to accept greater financial responsibility for training and retraining their workforces (Ainley and Vickerstaff, 1993).

Thus, corporatism in Britain represented a style of decision-making rather than a real contribution to the efficacy of economic policy. It sometimes looked as if permanent concessions were being given, particularly to the trade unions under the Labour governments of 1974–79, in return for promises of cooperation which turned out to be of little real value, as in the 'Winter of Discontent' of 1978–79 (see Appendix 1).

CONSERVATIVE GOVERNMENT, 1979–90

The incoming Conservative government of Margaret Thatcher set out to diminish the importance of both the TUC and the CBI.

For example, there was no more 'beer and sandwiches at No. 10'. The number of contacts at prime-ministerial level with the TUC fell off sharply after 1979, from nine in the last months of the Labour government in 1979 to one in 1980 and one in 1981 (Mitchell, 1987). The CBI also had a difficult relationship with government, leading its new Director-General, Sir Terence Beckett, to promise at its 1980 conference 'a bare knuckle fight' with the government.

The NEDC was downgraded in 1987. It met much less frequently, only four times a year, compared with the previous ten. There were fewer meetings with senior ministers, the Chancellor of the Exchequer chairing only one meeting a year, soon after the Budget. A number of industrial development committees were axed, 14 sector groups and 3 working parties replacing the 38 economic development committees.

The MSC was succeeded by the Training Commission in 1988, which was stripped of all responsibility for the government's new Employment Training programme after the vote for non-cooperation at the TUC conference.

As the then Trade and Industry Minister, Lord Young, said in 1988: 'We have rejected the TUC; we have rejected the CBI. We do not see them coming back again. We gave up the corporate state.'

CONSERVATIVE GOVERNMENT, 1990–97

Under John Major

there was a return to the more traditional style of policy-making in Britain. … civil servants remarked that they now felt more able to return to a previous form of intimate dialogue with groups, less fearful of a prime-ministerial dictat

Richardson, 1993.

However, there was no return to corporatism. It was Major who finally abolished the NEDC after his general election victory in 1992.

LABOUR GOVERNMENT, 1997–

'There are things that government, business and workforces can do together to make for high productivity', said the Chancellor of the Exchequer, Gordon Brown, in 1998, but 'corporatism was about people behind closed doors making compromises, not for the national interest, but to suit their own vested interests' (interview in *The Sunday Telegraph*, 26 July 1998).

The move away from liberal corporatism was not restricted to Britain. In the context of globalisation, few governments, of whatever political persuasion, were able to deliver their commitment to full employment 'which many have seen as the underpinning of corporatist exchanges between states, capital and labour' (Ainley and Vickerstaff, 1993). However, the collapse of corporatist structures was uneven. In those countries where such arrangements were strong, that is based upon established consensus, for example Sweden, the discrediting of corporatism was minimised.

THE DECLINE OF THE TRADE UNIONS

The membership of trade unions affiliated to the TUC declined from 12.2 million in 1979, or over 55 per cent of the workforce, to 6.8 million, or 30 per cent of the workforce, in 1997. A number of factors have been responsible for the decline in the role of trade unions since 1979.

CONSERVATIVE INDUSTRIAL RELATIONS LEGISLATION, 1980–93

Conservative governments after 1979 introduced a 'step-by-step' approach to legislation designed to curb what they saw as excessive trade-union power.

1980 Employment Act
- This made certain forms of 'secondary' action (that is action such as a 'sympathy' strike which was taken by workers who were not in dispute with their own employer) unlawful in most instances. It also made unlawful, organising picketing by workers, or workers picketing, other than at their own place of work.
- It weakened the closed shop (an agreement between an employer and a trade union requiring employees to belong to that union or another union named in the agreement). It also widened those groups of employees who could not be fairly dismissed for refusing to belong to a trade union in a closed shop, so as to include those who objected to union membership on grounds of conscience or deeply held personal conviction, those who were already employed when a closed shop took effect and had remained non-members since, and those who worked in closed shops introduced after the 1980 Act came into force and which had not been approved in a ballot by 80 per cent of the employees concerned.
- It introduced provisions for payments from government funds to be made to trade unions to reimburse the costs of holding secret postal ballots.

1982 Employment Act
- This made trade-union funds liable for damages in civil actions.
- It took further steps to undermine the closed shop: it made it unfair, from November 1984, to dismiss any employee for refusing to belong to a trade union in a closed shop if the closed shop had not, in the five years preceding the dismissal, been supported in a secret ballot by 80 per cent of the employees

covered by it, or by 85 per cent of those voting; it provided for compensation to be paid out of government funds to workers who were dismissed for refusing to belong to a trade union while pre-1980 legislation was in force; it increased the compensation which workers could claim from employers and trade unions for unfair dismissal as a result of a closed-shop agreement; and it made it unlawful to put clauses into commercial contracts which required that only union members be employed in carrying out the contract.

PICKETING WORKERS IN THE 1980s

1984 Trade-Union Act

- This required secret ballots for trade-union elections of union executives (though not general secretaries unless they held a vote on their executives).
- It also required secret ballots before industrial action to ensure that such action was lawful.
- It also required periodic 'testing' ballots of trade-union members with regard to the political levy.

1988 Employment Act

- This gave union members the right to apply to the courts for an order restraining their union from inducing them to take any kind of industrial action without a properly conducted secret ballot with majority support.

- It also protected individual members against unjustified union discipline, the most common example including going to work despite a union call to take strike or other industrial action; crossing a picket line; speaking out against a strike call or other industrial action; and refusing to pay a levy to fund a strike or other industrial action.
- It also extended requirements for trade-union elections of union executives to union general secretaries, presidents and even non-voting members.
- It also limited further the closed shop by providing that dismissal for any employees for not belonging to a union was now legally unfair, and by making it unlawful for unions to organise or threaten industrial action to establish or maintain any closed-shop practice.
- It also required trade unions to keep accounting records and make them readily available to union members for inspection.

1990 Employment Act
- This made it unlawful for an employer to refuse employment to job applicants on the grounds that they do not belong to a trade union.
- It also made all secondary or 'sympathy' industrial action unlawful.

1993 Trade-Union Reform and Employment Rights Act
- This made all pre-strike ballots postal ballots and subject to independent scrutiny.
- It also entitled employers to seven days' written notice of the intent of a call for any workplace disruption, and to identification of the workers involved.
- It also gave workers a legal right to join a trade union of their choice 'in circumstances where more than one union organizes employees of similar qualifications and occupations'.
- It also made the automatic deduction of union subscriptions from each individual employee's pay by their employer unlawful unless each employee provides written authorisation once every three years.
- It also provided customers of public services with the legal means to restrain unlawful action if an employer was unwilling to act or 'act quickly enough' in cases where 'the citizen may be defenceless' or when 'he is the specific target'.

CHANGING EMPLOYMENT STRUCTURES

- A decline in employment in manufacturing, which had traditionally been a trade-union stronghold.
- A rise in the share of jobs filled on a temporary, contract, or part-time basis – groups which are difficult to organise.
- A decline in public-sector employment, another area of union strength.

CHANGES IN THE ORGANISATION OF THE LABOUR PARTY

- *The selection of parliamentary candidates*. The introduction of 'one member, one vote' at the 1993 Party Conference curtailed the powers of the trade unions to select parliamentary candidates.
- *Elections of the Leader and Deputy Leader*. The trade unions' share of the vote in the Electoral College was reduced from 40 per cent to a third at the 1993 Conference.
- *The Party Conference*. The trade unions' share of the vote at the Party Conference was reduced from almost 90 per cent to 70 per cent in 1993 and to 50 per cent in 1995.

POLICY NETWORKS

The concept of **policy networks** stresses that relationships between pressure groups and government vary between policy areas.

The idea of a **policy community**, developed by Richardson and Jordan (1979), sees policy-making in Britain as taking place within a series of vertical compartments or segments, organised around a government department and its client groups, and generally closed off to the general public. They stress the interpersonal rather than the structured nature of relationships within policy communities:

The term 'community' was chosen deliberately to reflect the intimate relationship between groups and departments, the development of common perceptions and the development of a common language for describing policy problems

Richardson, 1993.

For example, the NFU and the British Medical Association (BMA) have intensive contacts with ministers and civil servants in the Ministry of Agriculture, Fisheries and Food on the one hand, and the Department of Health on the other.

The idea of a community does not imply an absence of conflict. Heclo and Wildavsky in their (1974) work on public expenditure decision-making note that

---

community refers to the personal relationships between major political and administrative actors – sometimes in conflict, often in agreement, but always in touch and operating within a shared framework.

Marsh and Rhodes (1992) distinguish between different policy networks which can vary according to the closeness of the relationships within them. Policy communities involve close relationships between pressure groups and government, while issue networks involve loose relationships between them (see Table 2).

Table 2: *Types of policy network:* *characteristics of policy communities and issue networks*		
DIMENSIONS	POLICY COMMUNITY	ISSUE NETWORK
Membership: – No. of participants	Very limited number, some groups consciously excluded.	Large.
– Type of interest	Economic and/or professional interests dominate.	Encompasses range of affected interests.
Integration: – Frequency of interaction	Frequent, high-quality, interaction of all groups on all matters related to policy issue.	Contacts fluctuate in frequency and intensity.
– Continuity	Membership, values and outcomes persistent over time.	Access fluctuates significantly.
– Consensus	All participants share basic values and accept the legitimacy of the outcome.	A measure of agreement exists, but conflict is ever present.
Resources: – Distribution of resources within network	All participants have resources; basic relationship is an exchange relationship.	Some participants may have resources, but they are limited, and basic relationship is consultative.
– Distribution of resources within participating organisations	Hierarchical; leaders can deliver members.	Varied and variable distribution and capacity to regulate members.
Power:	There is a balance of power among members. Although one group may dominate, it must be a positive-sum game if community is to persist.	Unequal powers, reflecting unequal resources and unequal access. It is a zero-sum game.

SOURCE: ADAPTED FROM MARSH AND RHODES, 1992.

REPRODUCED BY PERMISSION OF OXFORD UNIVERSITY PRESS.

A policy community has the following characteristics:

- There is a limited number of participants, with some groups consciously excluded.
- There is frequent and high-quality interaction between all members of the community on all matters related to the policy issues; consistency in values, membership and policy outcomes which persist over time; and consensus, with the ideology, values and broad policy preferences shared by all participants.
- All members of the policy community have resources, so the relationships between them are exchange relationships; the structures of the participating groups are hierarchical, so leaders can guarantee compliant members.
- There is a balance of power, not necessarily one in which all members equally benefit but one in which all members see themselves as in a positive-sum game.

An **issue network** is characterised by:

- the involvement of many participants;
- fluctuating interaction and access for the various members; the absence of consensus and the presence of conflict;
- interaction based on consultation rather than negotiation or bargaining;
- an unequal power relationship in which many participants have few resources, little access and no alternative.

SUMMARY

The traditional concept used to analyse the role of pressure groups in the political system is pluralism. An alternative concept is corporatism.

Britain moved towards a limited form of corporatism, or more accurately a weak version of tripartism, from the early 1960s until the end of the 1970s. The New Right critique of pluralism and corporatism was followed by the decline of corporatism.

The concept of policy networks has developed since.

STUDY GUIDES

Make sure you understand the concepts of pluralism and corporatism.

You should be able to explain the rise of corporatism in Britain, the New Right perspective and the fall of corporatism.

Know the concept of policy networks.

Answering essay questions on 'Pressure Groups in the Political System'

1 a Distinguish between the concepts of pluralism and corporatism.
  b How useful are they in explaining the relations between government and pressure groups in Britain?

You should be able to distinguish between the concepts of pluralism and corporatism. Recognise that pluralism and corporatism may apply more to some policy areas than to others. Offer alternative concepts (for example policy networks).

Answering document questions on 'Pressure Groups in the Political System'

DOCUMENT (BRITISH GOVERNMENT AND POLITICS)

Pressure Groups

Part of John Major's move in the direction of a more traditional form of Tory thinking appeared to involve a more tolerant attitude towards pressure groups. One of his first statements at Question Time urged the lobbies for and against Sunday trading to come to some kind of compromise solution which could then form the basis for legislation. This change of approach could be discerned at ministerial level. Contact between the leaders of the British Medical Association and the former Secretary of State for Health, Kenneth Clarke, broke down over the government's reforms of the National Health Service. His successor, William Waldegrave, offered to discuss the changes to general practitioners' contracts, including a joint effort to find ways to cut down on the paperwork involved. A joint working party on form-filling may not seem a dramatic breakthrough, but in fact it symbolizes a sea change in the relationship between the government and an important organized interest group.

The Thatcher approach to pressure groups seems, however, to have left a deep impression on the public mind, if not on Whitehall's working routines. John Major's promise to consult widely on the replacement of the poll tax was seized on by commentators and his political opponents as evidence of 'dithering'. Before 1979 that was how British government worked. Politicians might have bright ideas, but they were tested through an extensive process of discussion and evaluation.

Another sign of the reversion to the pre-1979 approach is the appointment of the Royal Commission to examine the criminal justice system, the first such royal commission since the Labour government. Various pressure groups will no doubt be giving evidence to the Commission, including the penal reform lobby. Mrs Thatcher thought that Royal Commissions slowed down decision making. No doubt they do, but it is a question of striking a balance between speedy decisions and decisions which are feasible and attract broadly based consent.

Even if a Labour government is returned to office, Britain is unlikely to revert to a more 'corporatist' style of decision making. In the 1970s an effort was made to manage the economy with the cooperation of the CBI and TUC. The centre piece of these attempts at government with the 'social partners' was prices and incomes policy. The Thatcher government frequently argued that 'corporatism' was one of the main causes of Britain's poor economic performance. This is a difficult argument to sustain because Britain never really had corporatism in the sense that it has been successfully practised in some smaller European countries such as Austria. The key to a successful corporatist relationship is the ability of the 'social partners' actually to implement the agreements they arrive at with government through their control over their own membership. The CBI and TUC in Britain were always too weak to be able to do this properly for any length of time.

Although the Labour Party advocates a closer partnership between government and industry, this does not mean full-blown corporatism. Rather, it means such steps as strengthening the role of the Department of Trade and Industry within government. The trade unions are unlikely to be sidelined quite as much by a Labour government as they were by the Conservatives, and one might expect to see the National Economic Development Council ('Neddy') restored to something of its former glory. However, many of the statements of Labour spokespersons stress the rights of individual workers, rather than their collective rights. This is part of a broader emphasis on the notion of citizenship which stresses a direct contractual relationship between the citizen and the state, rather than the role of 'estates of the realm' in looking after particular interests.

Professor Wyn Grant, 'Pressure Groups', *Politics Review*, Vol 1, 1, 1991.

---

2 a   What is meant by 'a more "corporatist" style of decision making' (lines 23–24)?

b   Explain the nature of the 'sea change' referred to in lines 9–11.

c   To what extent does the author suggest that corporatism in Britain failed before 1979 (lines 26–33)?

d   Using the article and your own knowledge, assess the changing nature of policy-making in Britain.

(University of Oxford Delegacy of Local Examinations GCE Advanced Level Government and Politics Specimen Papers and Mark Schemes, 2nd Edition, November 1995.)

3 a You should show that you understand the nature of government through 'social partnership', as it existed in the 1970s.

   b You should infer probably, but not necessarily, from the example given, that decisions were beginning to be taken on the basis of collaborative discussion rather than diktats from the Minister.

   c The major point here is that the author contends that corporatism did not fully operate before 1979. List accurately and comment on the attempt to manage the economy, showing how this system was deficient. Comment on why the system was deficient and what true 'corporatism' was.

   d Indicate the traditional role of pressure groups, the special position of the TUC and the CBI, the institutional arrangements by which these groups and others influenced governments, and governments' responses.

Practice Questions

1 Explain the rise and fall of corporatism in Britain.
2 Account for the decline in the role of trade unions since 1979.

4

PRESSURE GROUPS AND OTHER INSTITUTIONS

Introduction

THIS CHAPTER WILL look at how pressure groups relate to other institutions, including the executive, Parliament, the EU, political parties, the mass media, the judiciary and local government.

It will assess the extent to which the rise of the professional lobbyist is a cause for concern, and consider whether there should be a Register of Lobbyists.

The growth of parliamentary lobbying will be explained, the extent to which it is a cause for concern assessed, and whether there should be greater control over lobbying will be considered.

The extent to which, and why, pressure groups have increasingly concentrated their activities upon the EU will be explained.

Key Points
- Pressure groups and the executive.
- Pressure groups and Parliament.
- Pressure groups and the EU.
- Pressure groups and political parties.
- Pressure groups and the mass media.
- Pressure groups and the judiciary.
- Pressure groups and local government.

PRESSURE GROUPS AND THE EXECUTIVE

Pressure groups concentrate their activities where the power lies. In the British system, it lies in the executive, more so than, for example, in systems of government with a separation of powers such as the USA (see Simpson, 1998).

The core executive consists of

> *a complex web of institutions, networks and practices surrounding the PM, Cabinet, cabinet committees and their official counterparts, less formalised ministerial 'clubs' or meetings, bilateral negotiations, and interdepartmental committees*
>
> *Dunleavy and Rhodes, 1990.*

It also includes some major coordinating departments such as the Cabinet Office, the Treasury, the Foreign Office, the law officers, the security and intelligence services, and the Prime Minister's Office (see McNaughton, 1999). The executive also comprises other government departments, executive agencies and other governmental bodies.

Table 3: *'Based on your experience, place the following in order of importance in terms of seeking to influence public policy'.*[a]

SOURCE OF INFLUENCE	RANKING									RANK ORDER[b]
	1	2	3	4	5	6	7	8	9	
Parliament	7.6	11.7	29.2	17.0	11.7	9.4	5.3	5.3	2.9	4
Ministers	31.6	19.8	10.7	9.6	7.3	6.8	4.5	5.1	4.5	2
Civil servants/ govt depts	28.5	29.6	10.1	7.8	7.8	3.9	2.8	3.9	5.6	1
Political parties	4.3	4.9	12.3	9.9	14.8	14.8	14.2	17.9	6.8	8
One party in particular	6.7	2.7	8.1	6.7	6.7	10.1	13.4	14.1	31.5	9
Other interests or pressure groups	5.6	6.8	7.4	19.1	9.3	16.7	17.3	9.3	8.6	7
The media	20.6	10.0	14.4	15.6	18.3	7.2	9.4	2.8	1.7	3
Public opinion	9.5	11.2	8.3	11.2	7.1	14.2	13.6	12.4	12.4	6
Particular sections of public opinion	10.2	11.4	14.5	7.2	15.1	10.2	9.0	14.5	7.8	5

(a) Data are the results of a questionnaire completed by companies, interest groups and trade associations. (b) Calculated by scoring each ranking 1 for first, 2 for second, etc., the lowest total indicating first and the highest ninth. 27 respondents (10.7 % of the total) were 'don't knows' and 16 (6.3 %) said the ranking varied with the issue.

SOURCE: RUSH (ED), 1990A.
REPRODUCED BY PERMISSION OF OXFORD UNIVERSITY PRESS.

That the more important pressure groups have, and wish to keep, the majority of their contacts with Whitehall, that is the executive, rather than with Westminster, that is the legislature, is one of the better-documented generalisations in the study of pressure groups in the British political system. A survey conducted by members of the Study of Parliament Group, ranking various sources of influence, found that, on the basis of their experience, 58.1 per cent of pressure groups placed civil servants or government departments first and second in order of importance in terms of seeking to influence public policy, while 51.4 per cent placed ministers first or second (see Table 3).

A further survey asked pressure groups to rank various offices and institutions in terms of their perceived influence over public policy in general. Not surprisingly, the Prime Minister was identified by most groups as having the greatest influence over public policy. However, when the weighted scores were calculated, Cabinet ministers came out marginally on top, followed by the Prime Minister and senior civil servants (see Table 4).

Table 4: *Pressure-group ratings of offices/institutions in terms of perceived influence over public policy*

INSTITUTION/OFFICE	% OF GROUPS PLACING THIS INSTITUTION/ OFFICE 1ST	OVERALL/ WEIGHTED RANKING*
Prime Minister	58	2
Cabinet Ministers	23	1
Media	13	5
Senior Civil Servants†	9	3
Junior Civil Servants‡	3	6
Junior Ministers	1	4
House of Lords	1	9
Political Parties	1	8
Backbench MPs	–	7

* Overall rankings were calculated by weighting each group's top ranking by one, its second ranking by two, and so on. The office or institution with the lowest overall score therefore came top of this ranking.
† Senior Civil Servants = permanent secretary, deputy secretary and under secretary grades.
‡ Junior Civil Servants = assistant secretary and principal grades.

SOURCE: BAGGOT, 1992, P.19.

WHY THE EXECUTIVE CONSULTS WITH PRESSURE GROUPS

Advice

As government has become more complex, expert advice is needed. The government employs experts such as marine biologists, psychologists and vets. However, the government cannot have staff specialised enough to enable it to make policy and administer it without the advice of pressure groups. Advice here includes raw information, for example the statistical data which is essential to policy-making, and it also consists of technical knowledge and judgement (Beer, 1965). Government departments may be able to make use of the advice from pressure groups to press the departmental point of view with other parts of the government machine. For example, departments concerned with particular industries may use such advice to counteract arguments advanced by the Treasury. One large firm that was interviewed by Grant (1993b) recalled that they had been asked by the former Department of Industry to provide papers on such subjects as the impact of exchange-rate policy on industry, and the erosion of the industrial base.

Approval

The government also seeks the approval, or at least the acquiescence, of pressure groups, accepting that they have a right to take part in policy-making.

Assistance

The government may further require the active cooperation of pressure groups in carrying out a policy, for example of the BMA in carrying out changes in the National Health Service.

The need of the executive to consult with pressure groups is indicated by the formal obligation contained in some statutes. For example, the 1947 Agriculture Act, section 2(3), states that when holding reviews on the condition of the agriculture industry, 'the ministers shall consult with such bodies of persons as appear to them to represent the interests of producers in the agriculture industry'.

THE FORM OF ACCESS

The most usual distinction here is between formal and informal contacts involving pressure groups and the executive.

Formal contacts

The main formal contact is through advisory bodies. For example, surveys found that both the CBI and the TUC were each represented on over 100 of these bodies (Grant and Marsh, 1977; Marsh, 1983), and that 40 per cent of environmental groups also had representation on them (Lowe and Goyder, 1983).

Informal contacts

According to Grant and Marsh, the most important distinction in the form of access to the executive is that between bipartite and multipartite contacts. Most pressure groups prefer bipartite contacts which involve meetings of representatives of one pressure group with ministers and/or civil servants. They feel their case can be put and responded to more directly than in advisory bodies, where the government can 'play off' one pressure group against another.

Although the number of TUC contacts at prime-ministerial level fell off sharply after 1979 (see p. 18), meetings with ministers remained at the same level, between 60 and 70 a year, as under the Labour government of 1974–79.

There are few civil servants in the junior ranks of the higher Civil Service who do not spend some time of every day giving advice to, engaging in consultations or commercial negotiations with, or simply meeting representatives of, pressure groups in their area of responsibility (Miller, 1990). The survey by Baggot (1992) confirmed the high level of contact between pressure groups and the 'junior higher civil servants' (see Table 5). More senior grades are involved only if the stature of the issue or pressure group merits it.

Table 5: *Percentage of pressure groups in contact with institutions/offices over varying intervals*			
	% OF GROUPS IN CONTACT AT LEAST		
INSTITUTION/OFFICE	ONCE A WEEK	ONCE A MONTH	ONCE A YEAR
Prime Minister/PM office	1	11	53
Cabinet Ministers	8	37	81
Junior Ministers	11	49	86
Senior Civil Servants	19	50	82
Junior Civil Servants	34	67	85
MPs	31	61	89
Peers	18	50	84
Media	81	94	98

SOURCE: BAGGOT, 1992, P.19.

THE RISE OF THE PROFESSIONAL LOBBYIST

Professional lobbyist means 'someone who is professionally employed to lobby on behalf of clients or who advises clients on how to lobby on their own behalf' (Third Report from the Select Committee on Members' Interests, 1991, HC 586). Although professional lobbyists have been a feature of the British policy-making process since the late 1940s, the emergence of a wider professional lobbying industry in the 1980s and 1990s represented a new development in British pressure-group activity.

Lobbying company services can be basically divided into two distinct, though related, areas. First, all lobbyists offer a monitoring and information service. Second, and more important, lobbyists offer a range of opinion-forming services, aimed at directly influencing civil servants and legislators. In the larger public relations companies, direct lobbying programmes are often an integral part of a wider public relations strategy, involving relations with the media.

Typically, professional lobbyists draw their staff from an established pool of people with experience of the political system, such as former civil servants, former ministers and former political advisers. What these groups have in common is not simply their knowledge of the political process but also their ability to provide contacts. Despite all of the claims to provide a professional service, therefore, a great deal of lobbying activity is based on the churning of existing contacts and friends within the political system.

A cause for concern?

The professional lobbyists' claim to have inside access to civil servants and ministers has given particular cause for concern. Access to civil servants often results from the assiduous gathering of contacts over a number of years. In particular, the flow of experienced civil servants into lobbying companies has raised allegations of a 'revolving door' policy. Appropriate expertise, in addition to the prospect of enhanced access to the government decision-making process, is highly prized by commercial lobbying companies. Civil servants may be influenced by the lure of lucrative outside employment. Baggot's (1992) survey revealed that almost half of the pressure groups had within their organisation former civil servants working in a paid or honorary capacity (see Table 6).

Table 6: *Percentage of pressure groups having within their organisation various civil servants, ministers and peers*	
	% OF GROUPS HAVING WITHIN THEIR ORGANISATION
Former civil servants	47
Former ministers	9
Former MPs	17
Current MPs	27
Current peers	34

SOURCE: BAGGOT, 1992, P.20.

Rules on the acceptance of outside appointments by civil servants

The Business Appointments Rules are set out in the Civil Service Management Code. They provide for the scrutiny of appointments which former civil servants propose to take up in the first two years after they leave the service. To provide an independent element in the process of scrutiny, the Advisory Committee on Business Appointments is appointed by the Prime Minister, comprising people with experience of the relationships between the Civil Service and the private sector. The Committee gives advice on applications at the most senior levels, and reviews a wider sample in order to ensure consistency and effectiveness. The aim of the rules is in particular to avoid any suspicion that the advice and decisions of a serving civil servant might be influenced by the hope or expectation of future employment with a particular firm or organisation; or to avoid the risk that a particular firm might gain an improper advantage over its competitors by employing someone who, in the course of their official duties, has had access to technical or other information which their competitors might legitimately regard as their own trade secrets, or to information relating to proposed developments in government policy which may affect that firm or its competitors.

Most senior civil servants must apply for government approval. Applications for approval must also be made by civil servants who have had any official dealings with their prospective employer during the last two years of employment; or who have had official dealings of a continued or repeated nature with their prospective employer at any time during their period of employment; or who have had access to commercially sensitive information belonging to competitors of their prospective employer in the course of their official duties; or whose official duties during the last two years of employment have involved advice or decisions benefiting their prospective employer, or have involved developing policy, knowledge of which might be of benefit to the prospective employer; or who are to be employed on a consultancy basis and have had any dealings of a commercial nature with outside bodies or organisations in their last two years of employment. The rules do not apply to unpaid appointments in non-commercial organisations, ministerial appointments or, in the case of part-time staff, appointments held with government agreement while they were civil servants. Special advisers are subject to the rules in the same way as other civil servants unless they are offered a post by some employer which they left on being appointed as advisers, and remain there for two years.

Applications under these rules are either approved unconditionally or subject to conditions which may apply for up to two years. Conditions may include a waiting period before taking up the appointment; if the Advisory Committee believes that the appointment is unsuitable, it may add that advice to its recommendation that the application be subject to a waiting period of two years, and that advice will be available for publication.

There has also been concern over ministers who, on leaving office, take positions in organisations with which they have had official dealings. Ministers have the opportunity while in government to take decisions which may favour or disadvantage outside bodies.

The acceptance of appointments outside government by outgoing ministers

On leaving office, ministers should seek advice from the independent Advisory Committee on Business Appointments about any appointments they wish to take up within two years of leaving office, other than unpaid appointments in non-commercial organisations or government appointments. If the Advisory Committee considers that an appointment could lead to public concern that the statements and decisions of the minister, when in government, have been influenced by the hope or expectation of future employment with the firm or organisation concerned, or that an employer could make improper use of official information to which a former minister has had access, it may recommend a delay of up to two years before the appointment is taken up; or that for a similar period the former minister should stand aside from certain activities of the employer.

OUTGOING MINISTERS: ACCEPTANCE OF APPOINTMENTS OUTSIDE GOVERNMENT

129.   On leaving office Ministers should seek advice from the independent Advisory Committee on Business Appointments about any appointments they wish to take up within two years of leaving office, other than unpaid appointments in non-commercial organisations or appointments in the gift of the Government, such as Prime Ministerial appointments to international organisations. Although it is in the public interest that former Ministers should be able to move into business or other areas of public life, it is equally important that there should be no cause for any suspicion of impropriety about a particular appointment. If therefore the Advisory Committee considers that an appointment could lead to public concern that the statements and decisions of the Minister, when in Government, have been influenced by the hope or expectation of future employment with the firm or organisation concerned, or that an employer could make improper use of official information to which a former Minister has had access, it may recommend a delay of up to two years before the appointment is taken up, or that for a similar period the former Minister should stand aside from certain activities of the employer.

Ministerial Code – a Code of Conduct and Guidance on Procedures for Ministers,
Cabinet Office, July 1997.

Cash for access

In June 1998, journalists from *The Observer*, posing as representatives of US energy companies, asked lobbyists what they would receive if they bought their services. Derek Draper, director of lobbyists GPC Market Access (GPC) and adviser before the 1997 General Election to Peter Mandelson (coordinator of government policy at the Cabinet Office in June 1998), told them: 'There are 17 people who count. And to say I am intimate with every one of them is the understatement of the century.' The next evening, at the GPC's annual champagne reception at the Banqueting House in Whitehall, Roger Liddle, in charge of European Affairs for the Prime Minister's Policy Unit, handed *The Observer* journalists a card with his Downing Street and home phone numbers and said to them: 'Whenever you are ready, just tell me what you want, who you want to meet, and Derek and I will make the call for you.' Until the 1997 General Election, Liddle had been managing director of Prima Europe, the firm Draper worked for. Other lobbyists formerly working for the Labour Party were approached. Karl Milner, an adviser before the 1997 General Election to Gordon Brown (Chancellor of the Exchequer), and now a lobbyist with GJW Government Relations (GJW), faxed a House of Commons Select Committee report to the USA a day before publication.

LABOUR DENY CLAIMS OF SLEAZE AS A TURNSTILE IS FITTED TO THE ENTRANCE TO No.10......

PLEASE PAY HERE

PRIESTLEY 7-7-98

SOURCE: INDEPENDENT, 7TH JULY 1998

However, as Jordan (1989) writes, 'we need to weigh the impact not count the claims.'

RIGHT OF REPLY, MARK OATEN

The former managing director of a lobbying firm, now a Liberal Democrat MP, defends their role

I am not sure if poacher-turned-gamekeeper best describes my change from director of a lobbying consultancy to MP, but it does give me the chance to see both sides in this week's cash-for-access row.

The most telling remark has come from the central figure. When Derek Draper describes himself as being "boastful and brash" he goes a long way to describing the industry he works in. The reality behind the big-bills-and-sleaze image is that, sadly, most clients are all too easily satisfied with a fast-talking consultant who can impress with basic knowledge of the system. Throw in a few tit-bits suggesting you're an insider and sell it with the kind of skills Mr Draper demonstrates, and you have a happy client.

Early in my career I remember just how impressed Japanese clients were when sections from Hansard were retyped on fancy paper and marketed as "political intelligence". Frankly, this kind of service does not warrant legislation but more demanding relations between clients and customers.

This current debate seems to me to be about favours for friends. Working in a political party builds up associations and loyalties. If one friend ends up in Westminster, it is inevitable that favours will take place.

It is clear that lobbying falls into two categories: the who-you-know approach, which is not illegal but is unwelcome, and the winning-the-argument approach which, if undertaken professionally, can help.

Fortunately, the worst days of MPs being paid as directors of lobbying firms are over. It seems to me almost impossible to legislate against friendship between super-egos.

Independent, 9 July 1998.

Proposal for a Register of Lobbyists

Nevertheless, there is sufficient cause for concern for a Register of Lobbyists to be proposed to provide greater transparency and public accountability.

However, as the Nolan Committee's First Report on Standards in Public Life, 1995, stated, 'It is the right of everyone to lobby Parliament and Ministers' (Nolan Committee, 1995).

The greatest experience of a Register of Lobbyists is found in the USA. It has not been conspicuously successful, either at federal or state levels. A major problem is that most efforts, understandably perhaps given the greater importance of the legislative power in the USA, have concentrated on Congress (the federal legislature) and the State legislatures. The executive branches are largely ignored.

A Register of Lobbyists also raises questions of access and openness. For example, the Lobby Act in the USA requires lobbyists to register their activities on Capitol Hill, and to make subsequent quarterly statements detailing expenditures over the preceding three months. In practice, however, approximately half of the lobbyists in Washington D.C. fail to register (Berry, 1992a).

Less-than-scrupulous firms in the USA have led would-be clients to believe that being on the register bestows official recognition, even approval. As the First Nolan Report put it:

> *To establish a public register of lobbyists would create the danger of giving the impression, which would no doubt be fostered by lobbyists themselves, that the only way to approach successfully Members or Ministers was by making use of a registered lobbyist. This would set up an undesirable hurdle, real or imagined, in the way of access.*

It rejected the concept of giving lobbyists formal status through a statutory register, though it commended the efforts of lobbyists in developing their own codes of practice.

The Association of Professional Political Consultants

Leading lobbying firms set up in 1995 an Association of Professional Political Consultants (APPC), developing their own codes of practice.

In July 1998, the APPC concluded that GPC and GJW had both committed 'clear breaches' of the Association's code of conduct. GPC was guilty of 'action by an employee which had brought the industry into disrepute'. Mike Burrell, on the APPC's management committee, said GJW had committed a 'clear and acknowledged breach of Parliamentary privilege'. Representatives of the two lobbying firms told the Associations that they had taken steps to stop such breaches occurring again. They acceded to requests that they should withdraw from membership of APPC, pending an 'audit' of their new procedures.

Later in the month, the report of an inquiry, commissioned by APPC, written by Lord Armstrong, the former head of the Civil Service, and Nicholas Purnell QC, concluded that GPC and GJW had acted properly. Draper's claims marked a 'serious breach' of the APPC's code of conduct, and GPC accepted that he had 'brought the profession into disrepute'. However, Draper was a 'rogue elephant' whose conduct 'was to be attributed not to defects in management systems or procedures but to human failure'. Milner's action was 'an isolated incident'. Both firms had tightened procedures and were readmitted to the Association.

The report questioned the suitability of lobbying companies employing former political advisers, saying that they should be put on probation for three months to see if they could hold down their jobs. It called for all lobbying firms to be brought into the Association and to be subject to the code. Otherwise, it warned, the government would 'sooner or later' establish a statutory register with rules of conducts.

Guidance for civil servants: contact with lobbyists

On 27 July 1998, the Blair government published guidance for all civil servants, including special advisers, setting out the basic principles which should be followed in any contacts with people outside government, including lobbyists. The government's approach, reflecting the approach of the Nolan Committee on Standards in Public Life in its first report, 1995 (see p. 37), was not to ban contacts between civil servants and lobbyists but

---

to insist that wherever and whenever they take place they should be conducted in accordance with the Civil Service Code, and the principles of public life set out by the Nolan Committee.

This meant that civil servants could meet lobbyists, formally and informally, where this was justified by the needs of government.

Basic principles set out in the *Civil Service Code* include civil servants conducting themselves with integrity and honesty; not misusing their official position or information acquired in the course of their official duties to further their own or others' private interests; not receiving benefits of any kind which others might reasonably see as compromising their personal judgement or integrity; and not without authority disclosing official information which has been communicated in confidence in government or received in confidence from others. The principles of public life set down by the Nolan Committee as particularly relevant were as follows:

- *Selflessness:* holders of public office should take decisions solely in terms of the public interest. They should not do so in order to gain financial or other material benefits for themselves, their family, or their friends.
- *Integrity:* holders of public office should not place themselves under any financial or other obligation to outside individuals or organisations that might influence them in the performance of their official duties.
- *Honesty:* holders of public office have a duty to declare any private interests relating to their public duties, and to take steps to resolve any conflicts in a way that protects the public interest.

What the principles meant in practice would depend on the circumstances of each case. Some things were completely unacceptable, for example leaking confidential or sensitive material, especially market-sensitive material, to a lobbyist; or deliberately helping a lobbyist to attract business by arranging for clients to have privileged access to ministers or undue influence on policy. These would be serious disciplinary offences, and would trigger procedures under which civil servants would be liable to dismissal.

Much more common were grey areas where common sense had to be used. Here again, breaking the basic rules might lead to disciplinary action. For example, civil servants should not do anything which might breach parliamentary privilege or offend against the conventions of Parliament, remembering that the papers and reports of select committees are the property of the committee and subject to parliamentary privilege; or offer, or give the impression of offering, a lobbyist preferential access to ministers or civil servants.

The guidance concluded that lobbyists were a feature of our democratic system. There was no ban on civil servants having dealings with them where this served a proper purpose and was conducted in a proper manner. However, the need for propriety was crucial. Lobbyists themselves were bound to want to talk up their own influence and contacts. It was the job of all civil servants to make sure that they conducted their dealings with lobbyists in a manner which was proper and not open to misinterpretation.

PRESSURE GROUPS AND PARLIAMENT

The Study of Parliament Group survey found that pressure groups are mostly well aware of where the power lies. Only 19.3 per cent placed Parliament first or second in ranking sources of influence in order of importance (see Table 3 on p. 29). The findings of this survey were confirmed by Baggot's (1992) survey, the low assessment of Parliament's influence relative to other offices and institutions being quite clear (see Table 4 on p. 30).

THE GROWTH OF PARLIAMENTARY LOBBYING

However, far from being neglected by pressure groups, Parliament is subjected to much lobbying by them. The Study of Parliament Group survey found that 75 per cent of pressure groups had regular or frequent contact with MPs and that 59 per cent had regular or frequent contact with peers (see Table 7).

Table 7: *Pressure-group contact with Parliament*		
TYPE OF CONTACT	%	NO.
Regular or frequent contact with MPs	74.7	189
Presented written evidence to a select committee	65.6	186
Regular or frequent contact with peers	58.7	148
Presented oral evidence to a select committee	49.0	124
Contacts with all-party groups	47.6	120
Contacts with party subject groups or committees	40.9	103

SOURCE: RUSH (ED), 1990A.
REPRODUCED BY PERMISSION OF OXFORD UNIVERSITY PRESS.

Baggot's (1992) survey confirms these findings. Over 60 per cent of the pressure groups were in contact with MPs at least once a month, almost a third were in contact at least once a week, and half were in contact with peers at least once a month (see Table 5).

Parliamentary lobbying also increased in the 1980s. Baggot's survey shows that 45 per cent of pressure groups perceived an increase in contact with the House of Commons, only 4 per cent a decrease; and 37 per cent an increase in contact with the House of Lords, and only 5 per cent a decrease (see Table 8).

Table 8: *Contact between pressure groups and parliamentary powers*		
LEVEL OF CONTACT	% OF GROUPS PERCEIVING CHANGE AT THIS LEVEL OF CONTACT		
	NO CHANGE	DECREASE	INCREASE
Prime Minister	59	24	17
Cabinet Ministers	48	17	37
Civil Servants	47	7	45
House of Commons	51	4	45
House of Lords	58	5	37
European Community	36	4	60

SOURCE: BAGGOT, 1992, P.20.

Why Parliament is subjected to much lobbying by pressure groups

According to Rush (1990a), three explanations suggest themselves:

1 *It is simply a case of misperception.* Pressure groups have a largely inaccurate perception of Parliament's place in the policy-making process and really think that political power is centred in Parliament rather than government.

   Some pressure groups do labour under the misperception that Parliament holds the key to influencing public policy, but most are, as we have seen, largely in touch with the reality of where power normally lies.

2 *Parliament is used only when pressure has failed elsewhere and the normal consultation process has not produced the desired result, leaving Parliament as the last resort.* Failure in the executive may well lead to Parliament. For example, contact between what Baggot classifies as labour groups (that is trade unions and professional bodies) and the government was reduced in the 1980s. The largest increase in pressure groups perceiving an increase in contact with the House of Commons was amongst labour groups (Baggot, 1992).

However, this alone does not explain Parliament's role in pressure politics. Insider groups are more active than outsider groups in virtually every form of parliamentary contact. The Study of Parliament Group survey found that a greater proportion of insider groups (86 per cent) had regular or frequent contact with MPs, compared with outsider groups (67 per cent); and that 64 per cent of insider groups had regular or frequent contact with peers, compared with 55 per cent of outsider groups (see Table 9).

Table 9: *Contacts with Parliament by insider/outsider status*				
	INSIDER		OUTSIDER	
TYPE OF CONTACT	%	n	%	n
Regular or frequent contact with MPs	85.8	9	66.7	58
Presented written evidence to a select committee	83.0	88	53.1	78
Regular or frequent contact with peers	64.1	68	54.7	80
Presented oral evidence to a select committee	73.6	78	31.8	46
Contacts with all-party groups	51.9	55	44.5	65
Contacts with party subject committees	54.7	58	30.8	45

SOURCE: JUDGE, 'PARLIAMENT AND INTEREST REPRESENTATION', IN RUSH (ED), 1990A. REPRODUCED BY PERMISSION OF OXFORD UNIVERSITY PRESS.

Baggot's survey also showed that insider groups have more frequent contact with Parliament than do outsider groups. 72 per cent of insider groups are in contact with the House of Commons on a monthly basis, compared with 51 per cent of outsider groups, and 39 per cent in contact on a weekly basis, compared to 20 per cent of outsider groups; 63 per cent of insider groups were in contact with the House of Lords on a monthly basis, compared to 36 per cent of outsider groups, and 23 per cent in contact on a weekly basis, compared to 8 per cent of outsider groups (see Table 10).

Moreover, pressure politics should not be locked into a simplistic linear policy-making model which assumes that it involves seeking to make a *direct* impact on those involved at each stage. Much effort undoubtedly is made to exert direct pressure, but pressure can be, and often is, indirect also.

Table 10: *Contact between insider/outsider groups and parliamentary powers*				
	% OF GROUPS IN CONTACT ON A WEEKLY/MONTHLY BASIS			
	WEEKLY		MONTHLY	
	OUTSIDER	INSIDER	OUTSIDER	INSIDER
Prime Minister	–	2	10	14
Cabinet Ministers	5	12	37	45
Junior Ministers	10	14	38	67
Senior Civil Servants	12	25	45	49
Junior Civil Servants	12	55	62	76
House of Commons	20	39	51	72
House of Lords	8	23	36	63
Political Parties	13	27	34	51
Media	74	86	84	94

SOURCE: BAGGOT, 1992, P.20.

3   *Parliament really does have an impact on policy.* If a pressure group believes that representation through Parliament may have an effect, not necessarily excluding but in addition to other efforts, then it is likely to act on that belief. Certainly, Parliament may be seen as a last resort or as an opportunity to hedge bets. However, there is also much to be said for operating on a broader front, hoping that MPs, peers and, when appropriate, select committees, party committees and all-party groups will add to any pressure exerted directly on the policy process.

Private members' legislation

That the time and attention devoted to private members' bills is limited is clear from the public record. The House of Commons spends less than five per cent of its time considering such legislation (Norton, 1990). The time itself is usually concentrated in the least attractive part of the parliamentary week (that is Fridays), when MPs prefer to be in their constituencies. An MP needs to come in the top six names drawn from the annual ballot to have a realistic chance of having a bill debated.

Despite such limitations, private members' legislation has significance for pressure groups. It offers the opportunity to promote rather than resist change. Hence, this is one area of parliamentary activity where pressure groups are essentially proactive rather than reactive. Between five and fifteen private members' bills are likely to reach the statute book in any one session. Though precluded from imposing a charge on the public revenue, such bills can have an important impact upon public policy. Most notable instances derive from the latter half of the 1960s when major changes were wrought on moral issues: divorce, abortion and homosexuality as well as capital punishment. Such bills probably affected more individuals in their private lives than most government legislation.

Pressure groups will often help with drafting as well as providing briefing material. Parliamentary tactics will often be worked out in consultation with the pressure group (or groups), with members of the group being encouraged to put pressure on local MPs to support the measure. A number of private members' bills can be, and sometimes are, seen as being as much the bills of particular groups as of the sponsoring MPs. For example, Austin Mitchell's House Buyers Bill on conveyancing in 1983 was not only the Mitchell Bill but also a Consumers Association Bill, one of several credited to the Association and its legal officer, David Tench.

Private members' legislation thus encourages interest from pressure groups that is often intense. It is also broad. Of the three-quarters of respondents to the Study of Parliament Group questionnaire who had regular or frequent contact with one or more MPs, more than one in three (37 per cent) had asked an MP to sponsor a private members' bill.

Yet, in practice, pressure groups are even less effective in utilising private members' legislation to achieve legislative change than the limited time and attention given to private members' legislation would imply. There exists a restrictive filter. The filter is most restrictive at two stages in the process: initiation and deliberation. Though pressure groups are extremely and usually observably active in pushing for the introduction of private members' bills, only a small proportion of such legislation has its origins in pressure groups.

Private members' legislation provides a valuable, and fairly well-used, medium for introducing bills favoured by government departments but for which no slot is available in the government's parliamentary timetable. MPs who draw a place in the ballot can select such measures from a list supplied by the whips, and many do so. According to a study by Marsh and Read (1988), 18 per cent of balloted bills introduced in the sessions 1979–80 to 1985–86 originated in government departments, a larger proportion than in any previous postwar period. A further 23 per cent were found to have their origins in official, usually government committee, reports. The proportion of measures promoted by pressure groups was estimated at 23 per cent – a total of 25 bills in 7 sessions. Only in the period of the Conservative government from 1951 to 1964 had the proportion been lower.

The occasions when pressure groups manage to get a measure promoted through the medium of private members' legislation are thus relatively few. Furthermore, once introduced, the chances of success are less than those enjoyed by measures having their origins in government departments and reports. Of balloted bills passed in the period from 1979 to 1986, only 8 per cent – a total of five bills – had their origins in pressure groups. The reason for this disparity has been well summarised by Marsh and Read (1988): bills sponsored by pressure groups are 'often broad, non-technical and contentious'; whereas bills emanating from departments and official reports are 'narrow, technical and non-contentious'. The latter have, therefore, 'much more chance of passing and MPs, increasingly aware of the limitations of the procedure, have become more willing to introduce such bills'.

Once a pressure group has achieved the introduction of a bill, the longer and more contentious it is, the less likely it is to receive the Royal Assent. A contentious issue may fall foul not only of government but also of opposing pressure groups, who then lobby sympathetic MPs to oppose the measure. To achieve passage, bills need time, and that – on private members' days – is in short supply. For a contentious bill to achieve passage, its sponsor must therefore persuade both MPs and the government of the merits of the measure. Since the latter half of the 1960s, sponsors of contentious measures have been conspicuously unsuccessful in doing so.

This is not to contend that private members' legislation prompted by pressure groups does not serve some purpose. Merely by having a measure introduced and discussed, the sponsor is contributing to fulfilment of a limited 'tension release' function on the part of the House, allowing the issue to have a public airing. When moral issues in particular are discussed, the House becomes a focus for group activity and for the expression of views held by these groups. Even though not achieving passage, a bill may bring an issue onto the agenda of political debate and encourage the government at some later stage to introduce a measure on its own. On occasion, the threat of a bill being passed (or at least passing through most of its stages) against the wishes of the government may induce concessions on the part of the government. This happened, for example, with both Austin Mitchell's House Buyers Bill and Norman St. John-Stevas's bill which was enacted as the 1987 National Audit Act, creating the National Audit Office. Both bills had received second readings against the wishes of the Treasury bench.

For pressure groups seeking to effect a change in the law, there is thus some value in approaching MPs. Introduction of a private members' bill allows an issue to be raised; and there is even the possibility that it may eventually influence government thinking. The problem is that the opportunities here are limited.

Members of Parliament
Since 1970, MPs have proved willing, in a manner not experienced before this century, to exercise some degree of independence in their voting behaviour

(Norton, 1990). Governments have suffered significant defeats on the floor of the House of Commons and in standing committees on legislation. For example, the government was defeated on the second reading of the Shops Bill in 1986 (see Appendix 2). Standing committee proceedings produce more mundane but more typical examples. However, with majorities of the size won by the Conservative government in 1983 and 1987, it takes massive backbench dissidence to block or modify any government legislation. Thus, spectacular as it was, the defeat of the Shops Bill should be seen as an exception to the general rule that the government's will normally prevails in the House of Commons.

The House of Lords

The House of Lords has increasingly become a focus for lobbying. One of the salient features of the work of the Lords over legislation in recent years has been a growing assertiveness, involving not merely making drafting or technical amendments to legislation but also changing it considerably. For example, between 1979 and 1987, the Conservative government was defeated on 106 occasions (Baldwin, 1990). However, here, as in the Commons, the main thrust of the government's policies is seldom deflected.

Governments are not unwilling to make concessions on the details of policy, and it is details which are frequently the concern of pressure groups. On the other hand, many of the detailed changes made during the committee and report stages of bills in both the Commons and Lords are tabled not by backbenchers or by the opposition front bench but by the government itself, often as a consequence of behind-the-scenes representations to the government rather than through the intervention of an MP or a peer. Parliament thus becomes the vehicle for modifying policy rather than being the cause of it.

Select committees

According to Rush (1990b), in one sense, select committees are obvious targets for pressure groups, since through the evidence-taking aspects of their inquiries, they provide clearly defined opportunities for pressure groups to put their points of view across. In another sense, however, they appear less obvious targets: they have no powers of decision, do not deal directly with government legislation, and are by no means clearly defined channels of influence in the policy process, if indeed they can be said to be part of it at all. In fact, select committees have become a more significant focus for pressure politics as their numbers have grown and their activities increased.

The creation of a comprehensive select committee system covering all major government departments, which was completed in 1979, produced not only a more extensive range of select committees but also more select committee activity generally.

The increased number of committees inevitably meant more inquiries and therefore more opportunities for pressure groups to present evidence, but the departmental committees in particular hold proportionately more inquiries than their predecessors.

The development of the select committee system, however, was primarily concerned with strengthening the ability of the House of Commons to scrutinise the executive. Any opportunities such a system might afford pressure groups for being involved in the policy process were either secondary or even incidental to the main purpose. Accountability was seen as more important than participation, and least of all participation by pressure groups.

Select committees are essentially instruments of accountability, playing no direct part in the processing of government business, either legislative or financial, but they have the procedural freedom to choose their own subjects of inquiry and 'to send for persons, papers and records'.

The expansion of select committee activity has increased the number and range of inquiries conducted, but the number of topics covered in each parliamentary session is inevitably limited and is therefore a restricting factor in the involvement of pressure groups.

However, the power to take evidence is the key to the interest of pressure groups in select committees. Only the committees themselves can decide who is to appear before them, apart from the practical limitations of time, but anyone may submit written evidence, and many pressure groups have taken, and continue to take, the opportunity to do so.

In contrast to the House of Commons, the House of Lords has relatively few select committees. The Lords committees operate on a broadly similar basis to those of the Commons but are entirely independent of the latter. What is important for a pressure group is that they offer yet a further channel of access to Parliament, and, more particularly, that they complement rather than duplicate the Commons committees.

Pressure-group inputs to select committees

Although pressure groups contribute most obviously to select committee activity by the submission of evidence, there are other ways in which they can make inputs, especially in a less formal way. These are less easy to measure, but of their existence there can be no doubt.

The most apparent entails relationships with individual committee members; for example, Frank Field, the former director of the Child Poverty Action Group, was a member and then chairman of the Social Services Committee. Such contacts are useful but should not be exaggerated since there are limits to what individual committee members can achieve. Such members should not be seen simply as spokespersons or mouthpieces for pressure groups; they are more likely to be part of a two-way process between member and pressure group.

Ultimately, it is the committee members who decide the topics of inquiry, but their views are one of a number of factors. Most of them are beyond the control of pressure groups, but from time to time pressure groups are able to play an important part in the choice of topics.

Just as some groups have links with committee members, so links between both committee staffs and, to a lesser extent, the specialist advisers of committees have developed. The key member of staff of each committee is its clerk, who has general responsibility for the administration of the committee, assisted in some cases by a fellow clerk, and with a range of supporting staff. A select committee clerk usually stays with a particular committee for about five years and therefore becomes familiar with most aspects of the policy areas within the committee's remit. The clerk and other committee staff become known to group spokespersons and in many cases perform a valuable liaison role for their committee. The clerks' knowledge of their 'clientele' is invaluable to the committees, especially in deciding who can most usefully give evidence, especially oral, for each inquiry.

All the departmental select committees maintain extensive circulation lists for distributing information about their activities, including pending inquiries and calls for evidence. As the figures in Table 11 demonstrate, the proportion of pressure groups on each list varies considerably from 46 per cent for the Environment Committee to 3.3 per cent for Defence and numerically from a massive 113 for Transport to a mere 8 for Defence. This is partly a reflection of the varying styles of committees, but it is much more a reflection of the policy areas within their remits.

Being on a circulation list is neither a necessary condition nor, still less, a guarantee of being asked to give oral evidence. The opportunities for presenting oral evidence are inevitably restricted by the amount of time available. Deciding who should be asked to give such evidence is one of the early tasks when a committee embarks on an enquiry. In many cases, some of the choices are self-evident, but in others extensive inquiries and consultation may be necessary to find the appropriate witnesses. Written evidence may generally be submitted by any pressure group, but it is quite common for a committee to issue a specific invitation for written evidence from appropriate quarters. Moreover, pressure groups invited to appear before a committee are usually expected to provide a written brief prior to their appearance.

The pattern that emerged from the analysis of circulation lists is largely confirmed by the proportion of oral and written evidence submitted to the departmental select committees in the 1985–86 parliamentary session by outside interests. More than two-fifths of the oral and written evidence was generated by outside organisations, mostly pressure groups (see Table 12).

Table 11: *Pressure-group representation on the circulation lists of departmental select committees*			
COMMITTEE	%	*n*	TOTAL ON LIST
Agriculture	18.1	35	193
Defence	3.3	8	242
Education, Science and Arts	27.5	66	240
Employment	20.3	30	148
Energy	14.3	44	308
Environment	46.0	52	113
Foreign Affairs[a]	13.3	17	128
Home Affairs	16.6	34	205
Scottish Affairs	6.5	5	77
Social Services	25.9	42	162
Trade and Industry	18.4	19	103
Transport	30.2	113	374
Treasury and Civil Service	11.5	15	130
Welsh Affairs	7.7	14	181

[a] Based on an incomplete list, since part of the circulation list of the Foreign Affairs Committee is confidential and was not available for analysis.

SOURCE: RUSH, 'SELECT COMMITTEES', IN RUSH (ED), 1990A.
REPRODUCED BY PERMISSION OF OXFORD UNIVERSITY PRESS.

Pressure groups thus make a substantial input to the evidence received by select committees. Therefore, pressure groups provide the committees with a great deal of information and opinion and are a major source, for committees, of non-governmental information.

As shown in Table 7, 49 per cent of the organisations responding to the Study of Parliament Group survey had presented oral evidence to a select committee, and 65.6 per cent had presented written evidence.

Conclusion

The great majority (69.2 per cent) of respondents to the Study of Parliament Group survey believed that they had had some impact on the committee and its report (see Table 13).

Table 12: *Proportion of oral and written evidence submitted to departmental select committees by outside organisations, 1985–86*

COMMITTEE	ORAL EVIDENCE (%)	WRITTEN EVIDENCE (%)
Agriculture	55.6	57.9
Defence	23.8	36.0
Education, Science and Arts	66.1	55.8
Employment	41.4	55.5
Energy	55.0	54.8
Environment	37.4	40.8
Foreign Affairs	18.8	25.0
Home Affairs	30.9	25.6
Scottish Affairs	28.2	31.6
Social Services	64.9	61.9
Trade and Industry	49.5	51.2
Transport	42.6	37.5
Treasury and Civil Service	29.6	18.7
Welsh Affairs	9.4	42.4
Total	43.5	43.7

Information from committee reports and minutes of evidence.

SOURCE: RUSH, 'SELECT COMMITTEES', IN RUSH (ED) 1990A.
REPRODUCED BY PERMISSION OF OXFORD UNIVERSITY PRESS.

Table 13: *Impact of outside interests on select committees*

What impact do you believe your evidence made upon the committee and its report?[a]		
RESPONSE	%	n
Significant	16.3	28
Some	69.2	119
Minimal	8.1	14
None	4.1	7
Varied	0.6	1
Don't know	1.7	3
Total	100.0	172[b]

[a] This question relates to all respondents giving evidence to committees whether oral, written, or both.
[b] 2 respondents did not answer.

SOURCE: RUSH, 'SELECT COMMITTEES', IN RUSH (ED), 1990A.
REPRODUCED BY PERMISSION OF OXFORD UNIVERSITY PRESS.

The main impact is informational, but not merely for the committees.

Pressure groups also welcome the public platform that giving evidence presents, especially the opportunity to present oral evidence.

The informational and publicity roles are clear enough, but in so far as select committees can make recommendations, a significant proportion of which are accepted by the government, it is likely that pressure groups do have some more substantial impact on the policy process through select committees from time to time. One of the attractions of select committees for pressure groups is that they generally operate in a less partisan atmosphere than other areas of Commons activity. Divisions are not especially frequent and, when they do occur, are not always on party lines. Many of the recommendations made in committee reports concern the details of policy, rather than the principle, and the details of policy are what many pressure groups are interested in influencing.

Sometimes, there is evidence to suggest that pressure-group activity has had an impact on broader policy. Nonetheless, it would be naïve to expect a simple relationship between pressure-group input and committee output. Most groups are generally realistic about select committees.

Even so, the expansion of the committee system has widened the opportunities for pressure groups to seek to influence public policy through Parliament. Procedurally, select committees are largely an isolated part of parliamentary activity, but in the wider context of policy formation they are part of the policy network. Like other forms of parliamentary activity, select committees enable pressure groups to get issues aired, and even to secure a governmental reaction if any of their views are incorporated into a committee's recommendations. The specialised nature of the departmental committees allows a relationship to develop with some groups, to the point where suggestions have been made that a committee has developed too close a relationship in some policy areas. From a group's point of view, the giving of evidence, especially orally, confers a legitimacy within the policy community. Select committees illustrate perhaps better than more direct attempts to influence policy the amorphous nature of pressure politics: much group activity is directly aimed at ministers and civil servants, but much of it is also indirect, aimed at individuals and bodies who may in turn influence those, plus their advisors, who make policy decisions.

Miller (1990) lists the weaknesses of select committees as follows: 'Executive may ignore their work'; unlike Congressional committees in the USA, 'they don't handle consultation processes as a tribunal'; and they 'usually work too late to influence policy'.

Party committees and all-party groups

Introduction

According to Jones (1990), for those pressure groups seeking to influence political decisions, parliamentary parties are not so much hurdles as complications. They are neither monolithic organisations nor composed of free agents, but instead complex systems at the centre of which is a sensitive and frequently fragile relationship between the parliamentary leaderships and their respective backbenchers. The sensitivity derives from the delicate balance of loyalties which backbenchers have to maintain: to the leadership for career advancement and to their constituencies for political survival. The two are usually not at variance, but, depending on political circumstances, backbenchers may be either vulnerable or immune to outside pressures. This lack of certainty has encouraged a variety of pressure groups to direct at least a part of their activities towards influencing parliamentary parties.

The *party subject committees* have for some time been identified by pressure groups as important means of access to Parliament, and a similar rationale is evident in the attention paid to the *all-party groups*.

In the case of the party subject committees, there are higher levels of activity, regular weekly meetings, well-established schedules in the parliamentary timetable, and the development of specialised subcommittees. The all-party groups exhibit less structured characteristics and operate closer to the margins of the parliamentary system. Party lines are less distinct, and those pressure groups able to demonstrate the non-partisan nature of their case can expect to enlist the support of MPs from both sides of the House and to generate valuable publicity for their cause. That subject committees and all-party groups have become the focus of attention implies an expectation that they will be able to influence the policy process in Westminster. Yet this is by no means certain. Backbench committees, however well-organised and articulate, offer no guarantee of influence on their respective front benches. At best they are regarded as supplementary to other forms of pressure, and as an insurance if other avenues are closed.

Party subject committees

The party subject committees should not be too easily dismissed. An alternative view regards these committees as important, stresses their links with the Whips' Offices and party headquarters, and the option open to both Conservative and Labour committees to raise pressing issues at the weekly meetings of the 1922 Committee and the parliamentary Labour Party. Silk has concluded that through these committees backbenchers can force the leadership to change its policy on particular issues. For example, the former Secretary of State for Education, Sir Keith Joseph, withdrew his 1984 proposals on parental contributions towards student grants after opposition in the backbench Conservative Education Committee.

The unambiguous assertion of committee influence in this case needs some qualification. For the Conservative Party, the issue of parental contributions reverberated far beyond the confines of its education committee. Virtually all members of the Conservative Parliamentary Party were inundated by letters from enraged parents in what many MPs in retrospect regarded as one of the more awesome demonstrations of middle-class power. The committee may have been persuasive, but the evidence suggests that the vast majority of Conservative MPs were eager to be persuaded. Thus, particular circumstances applied which contributed to the 'success' of the committee in influencing its party leadership.

According to their chairpersons, the party subject committees' primary function is to liaise between front- and backbenchers and to maintain the morale and unity of the parliamentary party. Consultations with pressure groups, therefore, are incidental to intra-party negotiations. This could explain why only 40 per cent of the pressure-groups sample acknowledged any contact with party committees, as shown in Table 7 (see p. 40). This is not to suggest that pressure-group contacts with party subject committees are unimportant or unhelpful, but the lobbying process must take full account of the partisan arena within which the subject committees operate. Mandate obligations, ideological commitments, the latest public opinion polls, and the balance of power within the respective parliamentary parties may all, at various times and in different combinations, colour the mood of the party committees and the tone of the reception the pressure group receives.

While control is too strong a description, both main parliamentary parties consider it prudent to keep an eye on subject committees to head off any parliamentary embarrassment. Consequently, a pressure group concentrating on a particular committee disregards the wider parliamentary context at its peril. To be exerted effectively, pressure must be sufficiently subtle as to suggest that it is not in conflict with the broad thrust of party policy.

Despite the constraints, subject committees in both parties believe that they can contribute to policy-making. They look to the pressure groups to provide specialised information, invite their spokespersons to speak at their weekly meetings, make fact-finding visits, organise full-morning seminars on important topics to which various pressure groups will be invited to contribute, and hold joint meetings with other subject committees should the issue of concern cross committee boundaries. However, committee members harbour few illusions about pressure groups.

Committee members, without exception, have been confident in their ability to use the pressure group and to exploit its resources without compromising their integrity. The subject committees have regarded pressure groups as a resource which has enabled them to perform their parliamentary duties in a more professional manner.

All-Party Groups

In comparison with other parliamentary committees, the all-party groups have much to commend themselves to pressure groups seeking to influence Parliament. They are located largely outside established parliamentary power structures. Pressure groups enter and exit the parliamentary scene according to the enthusiasm and commitment of backbenchers, with little regard to the Whips' Offices. Indeed, the whips have little say in their deliberations, attend their meetings only intermittently, and then only as observers. An all-party group can perform several services, from asking Parliamentary Questions, either to elicit information or to generate publicity, to tabling Early-Day Motions as a means of identifying and recruiting additional supporters. Ministers are reluctant to deny access to delegations promoted by all-party groups, and the media tends to look less critically on a press statement which carries an 'all-party parliamentary' imprint than it does on one issued by an identifiable or self-proclaimed pressure group. At a more informal level, all-party group members can raise matters of concern in their respective party committees and, using the parliamentary network, detect early warnings of government legislative intentions. At the very least, therefore, pressure groups look to the all-party groups to stimulate parliamentary interest, to raise the political salience of particular issues, and, ultimately, to place them onto the political and parliamentary agenda.

It is doubtful, however, whether an all-party group totally dependent upon its own devices would satisfy the expectations of an ambitious pressure group. In the case of many all-party groups, outside help has taken the form of secretarial assistance. In 1988, of the 103 all-party subject groups, 25 had formal administrative secretaries or branch officers located beyond the confines of the Palace of Westminster. In some cases, the pressure groups' identity was openly indicated. For example, the Animal Welfare Parliamentary Group was serviced by the RSPCA. Pressure groups which provide secretarial assistance for all-party groups have numerous opportunities in the drafting of agenda papers, information 'packs', policy statements, and the précis version of official reports, to emphasise their particular viewpoint.

Interdependent relations

The party subject committees and pressure groups are interdependent, the parliamentary skills and political contacts of the backbenchers balanced by the research and information facilities made available by pressure groups. A similar relationship is present in the relationship between all-party groups and pressure groups, accentuated by the provision of organisational support without which many all-party groups could not operate effectively and some might not even exist. However, while the party committees and all-party groups are made use of by pressure groups, they are not the primary object of most lobbies' activities. The individual MP is the most obvious and the most frequently used parliamentary contact point, but he or she then acts as an intermediary between pressure groups and the minister, the department or the appropriate select committee; the all-party groups and party committees are important because they enable the intermediary role to be played more effectively.

Table 7 (see p. 40) shows that pressure groups have rather more contact with all-party groups than with party subject committees, but this might simply reflect the fact that there are many more all-party groups covering a much broader range of interests.

Outsider groups are more orientated to the all-party groups, they make more frequent contact with them, and they find them more useful than do the insider groups who tend to direct their activities towards the party subject committees.

Conclusion

While individual backbenchers and select committees are seen as more important by pressure groups, party committees and all-party groups have emerged as valuable intermediaries and facilitators.

There are two views of the role played by party committees. On the negative side, they are regarded as safety valves which help the party leadership inhibit backbench deviations. A more positive interpretation suggests that party committees are able to exert influence through their ability to exploit parliamentary procedures, to raise issues with ministers, and to lobby their respective parliamentary parties.

The all-party groups appear to provide more effective access points to Parliament for those pressure groups outside the political establishment or who seek to promote issues at variance with established values.

Party subject committees and all-party groups, because of their voluntary membership, are seen as potentially sympathetic to the 'message' which pressure groups seek to convey. At the very least, they provide a cost-effective method of distributing information.

Select committees, party committees and all-party groups are part of the wider policy community, or, to be more accurate, of a range of policy communities. None is the most important part of such a community, but they can play their part in setting the policy agenda, moving items up the agenda, focusing attention on specific and detailed policy concerns, and feeding information and opinion into the policy networks.

Rush (1990b) concludes that Parliament's role in pressure politics is a mixture of the direct and the indirect, sometimes contributing clearly to the policy-making process but more often part of the 'noise' that surrounds that process, at any stage of which the government may be influenced by representations made through Parliament as policy evolves. Moreover, Parliament's position as the representative body to which the government is constitutionally responsible confers a degree of legitimacy on representations made in and through Parliament, a body which thus has it attractions for pressure groups and, more mundanely, brings issues more fully into the public domain, itself a potentially powerful form of pressure should it attract the attention of public opinion.

A CAUSE FOR CONCERN?

The growth of parliamentary lobbying in general, and the use of professional lobbyists (see p. 32) in particular, have been a cause for concern. At the heart of this concern lies the financial relationship between lobbyists and MPs.

Parliamentary consultancies

There has been a significant growth in the number of MPs who had entered into consultancies or other forms of agreement which might reasonably be thought to influence their parliamentary conduct. Analysis of the 1995 Register of Members' Interests suggested that 26 MPs had consultancy agreements with public relations or lobbying firms, and that a further 142 had consultancies with other types of company or with trade associations. These 168 MPs held between them 356 consultancies. If ministers and the Speaker are excluded, there were 566 MPs. Thus, the Nolan Committee concluded that almost 30 per cent of eligible MPs held consultancy agreements of these types.

A similar, though by no means identical, relationship which existed for many years was that of sponsorship arrangements between MPs and trade unions. The financial support was generally limited to payment of a proportion of MPs constituency office and election expenses. There was no remuneration for the MP personally. Yet it was only natural that it should give rise to feelings of obligation which had the potential to influence the MPs conduct in the House. According to the 1995 Register, a total of 184 MPs (over 30 per cent of MPs excluding ministers) had sponsorship arrangements with trade unions. In addition, 27 MPs had paid consultancies with trade unions. A further 10 received other financial help from trade unions.

While the lack of detail in the Register made precise analysis difficult, it appeared to the Nolan Committee that in their different ways some 389 of the 566 eligible MPs, that is almost 70 per cent, had financial relationships with outside bodies which directly related to their membership of the House.

According to Berry (1992a), many MPs holding paid consultancies which relate to their parliamentary role provide very little in return for their fee. Indeed, it is unusual for MPs to do more than attend a monthly meeting known as 'prayers' where they report on relevant political developments affecting the interest or company. In short, MPs holding paid consultancies are expected to act as the lobbyists' 'eyes and ears' in Parliament.

Clearly, however, the nature of the relationship between an MP and a lobbyist may be open to abuse. Concern has been expressed that the activities of the lobbyists 'exert undue influence and ... operate to the exclusion of other, less well-organised and less well-funded points of view' (Doig, 1986). One area of concern is lobbyists' working for MPs as their research assistants. Lobbyists administering all-party parliamentary groups have also become a cause for concern. Jenny Jeger of GJW gave evidence to the select committee condemning those all-party groups which are serviced by professional lobbyists representing a trade association, as having only 'partial or preferential' interests, and cited an example of one of her clients being refused membership to an all-party group because it was believed to be a 'rival trade concern'.

Within parliamentary procedure, there are various ways in which individual backbenchers can raise interests in the House of Commons, for example by asking oral questions.

Cash for questions

In July 1994, *The Sunday Times* revealed that two Conservative MPs, David Tredinnick and Graham Riddick, accepted money for asking Parliamentary Questions on behalf of clients. Their cases were referred to the Privileges Committee of the House of Commons, which subsequently suspended them from the House for 20 days and 10 days respectively. Less than four months later, Al-Fayed, a prominent businessman and the owner of Harrods, claimed that on arriving in London, he had been informed that it was essential to hail an MP in the same way as one would hail a cab.

CONTROL OVER LOBBYING

The First Nolan Report

In October 1994, the Committee on Standards in Public Life, chaired by Lord Nolan, was established as a standing committee, which would remain in being to advise the government of the day.

The main recommendations of the First Nolan Report, published in May 1995, in the area of the House of Commons were as follows:

- MPs should be banned from selling their services to firms engaged in lobbying on behalf of clients. The House of Commons should set in hand without delay a broader consideration of the merits of parliamentary consultants generally.
- Full disclosure of consultancy agreements and payments, and of trade-union sponsorship agreements and payments, should be introduced immediately.
- A Code of Conduct for MPs should be drawn up. More guidance for MPs, including induction sessions, should be available.
- The House of Commons should continue to be responsible for enforcing its own rules, but should appoint a person of independent standing as

Parliamentary Commissioner for Standards whose conclusions and investigations and matters of propriety should be published.

- When the Commissioner has recommended further action, there should be a hearing by a subcommittee of the Committee of Privileges, comprising up to seven senior MPs, normally sitting in public.

Self-regulation post-Nolan

After prolonged study by the Select Committee on Standards in Public Life, the House addressed all the underlying concerns of the Nolan Committee but adopted solutions which differed from their recommendations in two respects:

1 *Consultancies.* The Select Committee concluded that the attempts of the Nolan Committee to regulate the *types* of outside bodies with which MPs should be allowed to have a paid relationship would not work because of difficulties of definition and enforcement. Instead, they identified the underlying concern that influence could be bought and sold through MPs, and concentrated on those *actions* which might be open to abuse or suspicion. They therefore distinguished between paid advice (permitted) and paid advocacy (prohibited).

In November 1998, the first Parliamentary Commissioner for Standards, Sir Gordon Downey, said in a memorandum submitted to the Committee on Standards and Privileges shortly before his retirement that to the best of his knowledge the financial links with lobbyists had been broken. The spectre of cash for influence through this route had fallen away. There was little doubt that the advocacy ban, coupled with the disclosure of employment agreements, had had a marked effect on the number of parliamentary consultancies. It was difficult to make valid comparisons when so many seats had changed hands, but the number of commitments involving the provision of parliamentary services had fallen by some two-thirds since the time when the new rules had come into force. He thought it was fair to conclude that the main concerns about influence being bought and sold had been substantially reduced.

2 *Procedures.* The Select Committee on Standards in Public Life broadly endorsed the Nolan Committee procedure for complaints but without reaching a firm view on public hearings. When it came to actual cases, the Standards and Privileges Committee rapidly concluded that the proposed procedure was not to their liking. In particular, it implicitly rejected the idea of a subcommittee. It therefore adopted, in effect, a practice under which the Commissioner established the facts and reached conclusions on rule breaches in virtually all cases. The Committee satisfied themselves, so far as possible, that proper procedures had been adopted and that conclusions were supported by evidence and were not manifestly unsound (a judicial review type function); and recommended penalties where appropriate. The House imposed the penalties.

Sir Gordon Downey said in his memorandum that cases might, of course, arise in future in which the Committee felt a full rehearing would be justified or where the appellant might have a right to a rehearing under human rights' legislation. It was therefore desirable that the Committee decide what appeal mechanism would be appropriate. Sir Gordon's own view was that this should, if possible, be an external panel, appointed by the House, on which a majority was apolitical. If lawyers were involved, its remit should be confined to resolving disputed matters of fact, leaving the House, through the Committee, to decide on the interpretation of its own rules. If, as seemed likely, bribery or corruption were made a criminal offence applying to MPs, he believed such cases should be tried in the courts. If they were left with the House, new procedures would be needed at both the investigation and appeal stages, importing the safeguards of the courts. This would be essential not only from the point of view of natural justice but also because it would almost certainly be required by the European Court on Human Rights.

PRESSURE GROUPS AND THE EU

POLICY-MAKING IN THE EU

The policy-making process within the EU is complex. In outline, the Commission proposes, the Parliament discusses, and the Council of Ministers implements, policy. The Commission and the Parliament are supranational bodies, while the Council is intergovernmental.

The **European Commission**, which meets mostly in Brussels, is often described as the executive branch of the EU because it monitors the implementation of laws adopted by the Council of Ministers. However, unlike the Civil Service in Britain, it has the exclusive right to propose legislation.

The **European Parliament**, which meets in Strasbourg and Brussels, is a forum of debate rather than a policy-making body. There is a democratic deficit in the EU.

The **Council of Ministers**, which meets mostly in Brussels, represents the interests of the member states. It finally decides on the legislation. *Regulations* do not require legislation, but *directives* always need secondary legislation on the part of national governments (see Davies, 1998).

Prior to the passage in 1986 of the Single European Act (SEA), most 'European' lobbying was conducted through national governments. This tendency reflected a concentration of decision-making power within the Council of Ministers at the level of the European Community, as it was then called. Since the Luxembourg Compromise of 1966 gave each national government a veto over proposals put to the Council by the European Commission, many pressure groups relied upon their Civil Service contacts to defend them at the European level.

THE EXPANSION OF EUROPEAN LOBBYING

In Baggot's (1992) survey of pressure-group views of changes during the 1980s, the considerable increase in contact with European institutions was particularly evident. Almost two-thirds of pressure groups perceived an increase at this level of contact (see Table 8 p. 41).

Why the expansion in lobbying?

According to Baggot (1995), there are three related reasons why pressure groups have expanded their lobbying efforts in Europe:

1 European institutions are increasingly perceived by pressure groups as having much more influence over domestic policy decisions than was previously the case.

As Mazey and Richardson (1993) argue, any British pressure group which continues to rely exclusively on lobbying Westminster and Whitehall is adopting a high-risk strategy, because on a large range of issues, policies are now being determined in Brussels. The SEA, which sought to move from a common market to a single, or internal, market (that is one involving the free movement of goods, services, capital and labour within the Community), transformed the position. Its impact was twofold:

1   The scope of Community policies was extended to include policies which were previously the responsibility of national governments, notably environmental and social policies.
2   Institutional reforms significantly reduced the policy-making influence of the British government in key policy areas.

Qualified Majority Voting (QMV), under which each member state is allocated so many votes depending on the size of its population, and where a certain number is required to approve a measure, was extended to new policy areas. This was accompanied by a diminution in the use of the above-mentioned Luxembourg Compromise. There appeared to be agreement among the member states that this should not be invoked with respect to those policy areas brought under the Community's jurisdiction for the first time, such as the environment. In addition, member states were generally reluctant to appear to be holding up legislation relating to the internal market. By reducing the extent to which national governments within the Council were either willing or able to obstruct proposals, the greater use of majority voting increased the incentive for pressure groups to seek allies in other member states in order to achieve either a qualified majority or a blocking minority.

The SEA introduced a new 'cooperation procedure' which granted the European Parliament the right to a second reading of all Community legislation relating to the establishment and functioning of the single market, social and economic cohesion, technological research and development, and certain aspects of

Community social and regional policies. This provided Members of the European Parliament (MEPs) with a further opportunity to propose amendments to the 'common position' adopted by the Council of Ministers. For pressure groups, the Parliament thus became a useful means of achieving amendments to Community legislation.

The Treaty of European Union, signed in 1991 at Maastricht, and often referred to as the Maastricht Treaty, extended further the competences of European institutions into areas such as public health and consumer protection, and further altered decision-making processes.

2 Pressure groups began to see European institutions as more accessible and receptive to their views.

Both the SEA and the Maastricht Treaty contributed greatly to this. The extension of the competences of European institutions created a demand, particularly from the European Commission, for the kinds of information and expertise that pressure groups are able to provide. As a result, it became much more open and accessible to pressure groups which could provide such assistance.

3 Pressure groups which lacked influence at home began to take Europe seriously as a means of challenging the British government's policies.

The results they achieved encouraged them to devote more resources to lobbying at a European level. Among these pressure groups were those which had been wholly or partly excluded from the decision-making process in Britain during the 1980s, for example the trade unions.

TRADE UNIONS AND THE EU

The trade unions had traditionally opposed European integration, seeing it as a 'capitalist club'. However, after the Labour Party's third successive election defeat in 1987, the trade unions, together with the Labour Party, began to change their attitude. Jacques Delors, under whom the European Commission had expressed fears that, when the economic and trade barriers came down in January 1993, member states would seek to gain unfair cost advantages by depriving their workers of basic entitlements, was enthusiastically received when he addressed the 1988 TUC. He was the architect of the Community Charter for Workers, 1989, the aims of which were 'the promotion of employment, improved living and working conditions, proper social protection and dialogue between management and labour'. The Conservative government in Britain opposed the Social Charter, as it came to be called, claiming that it was a 'Socialist Charter' which would 'let in socialism by the back door'. At the Maastricht summit in 1991, Britain opted out of the Social Chapter, which was removed from the Treaty, the other 11 states going ahead with it but outside the Treaty. The TUC's enthusiasm for the 'social partnership' implicit in the Social Chapter marked an acknowledgement that the EU, far from being a threat to British trade unionists' rights and privileges, might actually provide protection from the continuing legislative assault of a hostile national government.

Within two days of taking office in 1997, the Labour government made it clear that it would sign up to the Social Chapter.

Other pressure groups were unhappy with the policies of the British government during the 1980s, for example environmental pressure groups.

ENVIRONMENTAL PRESSURE GROUPS AND THE EU

The drive to create a single market widened the powers of the European Commission over environmental issues. The Maastricht Treaty extended the powers of the European Parliament over these issues. For example, the British government has been found inadequate in regard to the pollution standards of its beaches.

CHANNELS THROUGH WHICH PRESSURE GROUPS OPERATE AT THE EUROPEAN LEVEL

The British government

Even in a federal system like that of the USA, pressure groups use state governments to put pressure on the federal authorities. In the British system, pressure groups use the national government to put pressure on the European institutions. For example, the NFU uses the British government to put pressure on the Council of Ministers over such matters as the Common Agricultural Policy (which aims to stabilise agricultural prices).

Implementation of EU directives is in the hands of national governments. Use of the national channel at this stage may ease the pain of decisions that threaten particular interests. For example, according to Sargent (1993), damage limitation is the speciality of trade associations:

Damage-limitation activities may involve attempts to limit the scope of a particular piece of legislation, to exempt a category of companies altogether, or to remove from the scope of a proposal some of a company's most sensitive products. ... At other times, attention focuses on taking action to achieve as late an implementation date as possible, in order to avoid the consequences of being unable to meet the requirements of the original deadline.

Euro-groups

However, the changing power structure in Europe has inevitably caused a proliferation of lobbying in Brussels and Strasbourg. Baggot's survey (1992) found that around three-quarters of British pressure groups were in some way connected to a European-wide pressure group. Table 14 shows some of the more well-known Euro-groups. The staffing of the Union of Industries of the European

Community (UNICE) indicates the importance and wide-ranging nature of its activities. The principal umbrella organisation for employers, it has some 36 specialist working groups. The European Environmental Bureau (EEB) was formed in 1974 to represent national environmental groups at the European level.

Table 14: *Some of the leading Euro-groups*				
	HEADQUARTERS			
GROUP	FOUNDED	STAFF	MEMBERSHIP	OTHER INFORMATION
COPA Committee of Professional Agricultural Organisations of the EC	1958	Brussels 35	22	Main agricultural group. Several specialist working-groups, eg milk, tobacco, etc.
UNICE Union of Industries in the European Community	1958	Brussels 25	13	Main employers' group. Several working-groups, eg Industrial Affairs, Social Affairs
BEUC European Bureau of Consumer Unions	1973	Brussels 7	16	Main voice of the consumer associations. No permanent working-groups
ETUC European Trade Union Confederation	1973	Brussels 28	17	Main trade-union association. Some working-groups
EEB European Environmental Bureau	1974	Brussels 2	37	Lacks resources of more powerful umbrella organisations. No permanent specialist groups
FÉDÉRATION BANCAIRE Banking Federation of the European Community	1960	Brussels 6	10	Main voice of the commercial banks in EC. 3 specialist groups

SOURCE: WATTS, 1993, P.118.

European institutions

Direct contacts with European institutions have become increasingly important for many pressure groups, as the survey by Watts indicates (see Table 15). Almost all of the groups lobby members of the Commission, personally or by written submissions.

Some major pressure groups have set up offices in Brussels. Baggot's survey (1992) found that 12 per cent of pressure groups had established a European office. These offices were first conceived primarily as listening posts/service centres for members and staff attending meetings in Brussels. They have become a more significant part of the groups' activities in recent years. Brussels is the place for them to be, for not only is the Commission based there, but the committees and party groupings of the European Parliament also meet in the city.

Four EU institutions are the targets of pressure-group influence, namely the Commission, the Council of Ministers, the European Parliament and the European Court of Justice (ECJ), usually in that order of priority (Mazey and Richardson, 1993). For example, environmental groups monitor the implementation of directives and act as 'whistle-blowers' by 'warning the Commission of implementation failure at the national level' (Mazey and Richardson).

In 1991, Compassion in World Farming (CIWF) presented a petition to the President of the European Parliament, with over a million signatures from citizens in the 12 member states, to change the status of animals from 'agricultural products' to 'sentient beings' (see Appendix 3). The European Parliament in 1994 supported the recommended change in status, but amendment to the Treaty of Rome requires the consent of all member states. CIWF's campaign to change the Treaty gained the support of a coalition of animal-welfare groups, known as the European Committee for Improvements in the Transport of Farm Animals, formed in 1993. In the summer of 1996, at the Inter-Governmental Conference (IGC) in Amsterdam, it was unanimously decided by the 15 member states to recognise animals as sentient beings. The protocol annexed to the Treaty of Rome commits the EU to 'pay full regard to the welfare requirements of animals' when formulating and implementing policies on agriculture, transport, research and the internal market.

However, no pressure group can ignore the ECJ, sitting in Luxembourg. It offers another route for outsider groups. For example, in 1995, CIWF, along with the International Fund for Animal Welfare, challenged the prevention of trade restrictions banning live exports of calves on the basis of a clause in Article 36 of the Treaty of Rome which permits a member state to impose partial or complete trade restrictions if this can be justified on grounds of 'public morality, public policy, or public security; the protection of the health and life of humans, animals or plants' (see again Appendix 3). The case reached the ECJ, the first time that an animal

Table 15: *Findings of the questionnaire on lobbying*					
	Routes employed to influence EC				
Group	Lobbying British Gov.	Lobbying via Euro-Groups	Direct from Britain	Lobbying from Office in Europe	Importance of European dimension
The Business Lobby					
Confederation of British Industry	✓	✓		✓	Ever-increasing importance
Engineering Employers Federation	✓	✓	✓		Increasingly important
					Stresses British activities
Institute of Directors	✓	✓	✓		Growing importance
Society of Motor Manufacturers and Traders	✓	✓	✓		Becoming more important
The Union Lobby					
National Union of Rail, Maritime and Transport Workers	✓ (via MPs)	✓	✓		Great interest in Europe
					Sees need to extend activities there
Transport and General Workers Union	✓ (via MPs)	✓	✓		Becoming more important
Rural, Agricultural and Allied Workers (sub-division of T&GWU)	✓	✓	✓		Very important
					Active in European Landworkers Federation
Trade Union Congress	✓	✓	✓		Sees value in using ETUC
The Professional Lobby					
Law Society	✓	✓		✓	Sees need for outpost in EC
					Has members working there
British Medical Association	✓	✓	✓		Has become very involved
					Regularly uses EC machinery
The Animal Welfare Lobby					
British Veterinary Association	✓	✓	✓		Ever-increasing importance
					Very professional approach
Royal Society for Prevention of Cruelty to Animals	✓	✓	✓		Growing importance
					Regularly uses EC machinery
The Environmental Lobby					
Automobile Association	✓		✓		Emphasis strongly on Britain
Campaign for Lead-Free Petrol	✓				Little interest
					Europe already ahead of Britain
Friends of the Earth	✓	✓	✓		Active at European level
					Campaign strongly on water purity
Greenpeace	✓	✓	✓		Active in Europe
Of 20 groups surveyed, 16 responded.					

Source: Watts, 1993, p.118.

welfare organisation had been able to take its case this far. In autumn 1997, the Opinion of the Courts' Advocate-General appeared to indicate that Britain might be able to invoke Article 36 if there is scientific evidence that the veal-crate system does have substantial health problems for calves and that the British public has clearly expressed the view that the trade is morally unacceptable.

The British government has been forced to bring national legislation on pensions, social security payments and equal opportunities at work into line with European law. The ECJ overruled the British government over the Working Time Directive in 1997. The government had argued that the opt-out on the Social Chapter meant that the directive did not apply to Britain, but the Commission claimed that it was a matter of health and safety (governed by QMV) *not* of social policy.

PRESSURE GROUPS AND POLITICAL PARTIES

Political parties outside Parliament are another channel of access.

TRADE UNIONS AND THE LABOUR PARTY

The Labour Party told the Neill Committee on Standards in Public Life in its written submission that between 1992 and 1996 the proportion of the party's income coming from trade unions fell from 66 per cent to 35 per cent, rising to 40 per cent in 1997. Ms Margaret McDonagh, then the Deputy Secretary, said in evidence that 30 per cent of the party's income came from the trade unions (Neill Committee, 1998).

Political funds

In 1996, 42 trade unions maintained political funds, to which 4.9 million members contributed (Annual Report of the Certification Officer 1997). In its written submission to the Neill Committee, the Labour Party said that 26 trade unions were affiliated to it in 1996, to which 3.5 million members contributed. Forty-four per cent of the expenditure from all political funds went to the Labour Party in the form of affiliation fees. The remainder was spent on lobbying activities or on general political advertising, much of which is likely to support the Labour Party.

Donations

Eleven trade-union organisations gave the Labour Party more than £5,000 in 1997, either as a cash donation or in the form of sponsorship of party events. The following gave cash: the Amalgamated Engineering and Electrical Union (AEEU); the Associated Society of Locomotive Engineers and Firemen (ASLEF); the Communication Workers Union; the General Municipal Boilermakers Union (GMB); the Graphical Print Media Union; the Transport and General Workers Union (TGWU); Unison; and the West Midlands Trade Union Liaison

Committee. The following gave sponsorship: Amalgamated Engineering and Electrical Services; the Graphical Print Media Union; the Scottish Trade Union Labour Party Liaison Committee; the TGWU; the TU Fund Managers Ltd, a TUC investment company; and Unison.

Constituency plan agreements

Constituency plan agreements between trade unions and selected constituency Labour parties replaced trade-union sponsorship of MPs in 1995. They involve some trade-union money going to support constituency activities, in return for which the trade union has some representation on the general committee of the Constituency Labour Party (CLP). Some 100 constituency plan agreements were in place in the early months of the 1997 Parliament (Butler and Kavanagh, 1997). For example, Chris Pond, the new Labour MP for Gravesham, a key target seat at the 1997 General Election, received 89 per cent of election expenses from trade unions, £6,650 from nine unions out of a total expenditure of £7,479 (*Daily Telegraph*, 31 December 1997).

The organisation of the Labour Party

Changes in the organisation of the Labour Party has been one of the factors responsible for the decline of the role of trade unions since 1979 (see Chapter 3). However, in 1998, trade unions still had 50 per cent of the vote at the party conference. They had 12 of the 32 seats on the National Executive Committee which, subject to the control and direction of conference, is the administrative authority of the party. And they still had a third of the vote in the elections of the Leader and the Deputy Leader of the party.

THE PARTY CONFERENCE

Lobbyists have targeted the party conference for a number of reasons, not least for the opportunity it provides to address key party figures and to promote clients' interests to a captive audience.

Commercial lobbying involvement in the party conference has taken a number of forms, ranging from the presence of expensive exhibition stands throughout conference week to the promotion of fringe meetings by outside interests. For example, in 1998, 230 organisations paid between £3,000 and £8,000 for stands in the exhibition area at the Labour Party Conference in Blackpool, bringing in more than £1 million (*Independent*, 28 September 1998). There were 87 firms and pressure groups paying up to £5,500 each to rent exhibition space in the Brighton Conference Centre for the Liberal Democrat Conference, covering more than £2,000 of the total conference bill. Among those who paid the full rate was the Police Federation (*Independent*, 21 October 1998). Fifty-one organisations were booked to be at the Conservative Party Conference, paying about £7,000 each, and raising about £350,000. They included regular exhibitors since the 1980s, such as the Scots Whisky Association and Age Concern (*Independent*, 5 October 1998).

PRESSURE-GROUP PROTESTS AT PARTY POLITICAL CONFERENCES

However, the question remains as to what extent these techniques are effective in any meaningful way (Berry, 1992b). In many cases, there is a very real sense in which the burgeoning commercial lobbying presence at all party conferences represents little more than the need-to-be-seen-doing-something factor. This particularly applies to those many interests which use the party conferences as extensions of their general PR, advertising and lobbying campaigns.

Of course, pressure groups often do have a specific purpose to their conference activities, notably to overcome misconceptions or promote a more sympathetic hearing in the party concerned. For example, the Scottish Whisky Association maintained a high visibility at the Conservative Party Conference in 1991, as it had done for many years, principally to raise the issue of excessive duty levels imposed on their product. In more general terms, however, it is possible to argue that lobbying activity at the party conferences has simply become self-perpetuating and that many lobbyists attend because that is what is expected of them. Many functions are in this sense aimed primarily at renewing friendships and establishing new contacts on a social level, that is they have no serious immediate lobbying purpose. However, it would be mistaken to assume that this

represents the sum total of lobbying activity at the conferences. On one level, while many commercial lobbyists have claimed that attendance at party conferences is a waste of time, they nevertheless have admitted to organising events if it makes the client feel good. In this respect, the vanity and generally low level of political awareness displayed by many clients of lobbying companies can be a potent weapon in the hands of the unscrupulous lobbyist and should not be underestimated. Clients who enjoy being pampered and made to feel self-important can be easily satisfied during the conference season. Berry notes that one leading lobbyist had admitted that many of its activities at party conferences were largely cosmetic and might involve little more than ensuring that the client and the exhibition stand were photographed with an MP or even a minister, for example.

While much of the conference season is undoubtedly little more than an excuse for social gatherings, parties and the opportunity to renew old friendships, there is a more serious side to the presence of the lobbyists. Although cosmetic on one level, decisions to invest thousands of pounds in exhibition stands, or to host receptions and fringe meetings, are not taken lightly, and there is some evidence that exhibitors are now buying access to senior party figures.

PRESSURE GROUPS AND THE MASS MEDIA

THE ROLES OF THE MASS MEDIA

The two main forms of mass media which are most significant from the point of view of pressure groups are the press and broadcasting, the latter including radio and television. Pressure groups appreciate the role of the mass media in raising public awareness and building public support. The Study of Parliament Group's survey found that, based on their experience, one in five pressure groups placed the media first in order of importance in terms of seeking to influence public policy (see Table 3 on p.29). In Baggot's (1992) survey, a lower but nevertheless significant percentage of pressure groups, 13 per cent, placed the media first in ranking various institutions in terms of their perceived influence over public policy in general (see Table 4 on p.30). Baggot's survey also found that four-fifths of the pressure groups were in contact with the media at least once a week (see Table 5 on p.32); and that half had contact on a daily basis.

This has led to a professionalisation of the relations between pressure groups and the mass media. Most of the larger and wealthier pressure groups employ public-relations experts. Many employ ex-media personnel. People who have previously worked in the media not only have experience and knowledge of how the media work but also possess a wide range of contacts working in the media, often former colleagues, who can be helpful when the pressure group wishes to go public.

HOW PRESSURE GROUPS USE THE MASS MEDIA

Pressure groups use the mass media to establish a presence. They use natural disasters to launch membership drives. For example, Greenpeace

---

is regularly contacted by newspapers alerting them to advertising possibilities when an environmental story is about to be published. Thus, the group will advertise on the same page as a lead story and a picture of environmental damage or stricken wildlife

Jordan and Maloney, 1997.

Media exposure is especially vital to those pressure groups striving to highlight the nature of a problem, especially where the public authorities are reluctant to recognise its scale or even existence. Obtaining cover in the popular press and broadcast media is linked to the desire to effect a cultural change amongst the public generally, as well as to the attempt to secure a specific political objective. For example, the media exposure has been perhaps the most important tactic of the anti-organophosphorous (OP) campaign. Much of the protest has been directed at gaining official recognition that a problem exists. Coverage in the press and TV has been central to achieving the cultural shift sought by many of the critics of OPs (see Appendix 4).

Media coverage can reinforce a case being made to civil servants by demonstrating that the matter is one of public concern. It may help to move the problem up the political agenda. For example, Snowdrop collected around 705,000 signatures for tighter gun control, with a further 450,000 people signing *The Sunday Mail's* petition calling for handguns to be made illegal (see Appendix 5).

Issues are raised in many factual TV and radio programmes. For example, in 1997, a two-part *World in Action* documentary covered the wide range of OP use (see again Appendix 4). Pressure groups may seek to influence the content of productions in an effort to advance their cause. For example, perhaps the clearest sign of the way in which the debate on the issue of OPs in sheep dipping has seeped into the public realm has been its incorporation into episodes of fictional programmes such as the radio series *The Archers* and the TV series *Mortimer's Law*.

A topical issue often leads the media to the group rather than vice versa. This was seen in Dunblane, where the Snowdrop campaign was more or less adopted by the press (see again Appendix 5). Such an endorsement of campaigns by the media facilitates and enhances the building-up of public support.

Nevertheless, media publicity is essentially ephemeral in character, and the media's attention span on an issue is necessarily limited. Furthermore, obtaining media publicity can become a substitute for effective political action. The media publicity may actually be counterproductive because it could lead supporters among the public into thinking that nothing needs to be done. For example,

'Watching a handful of heroic Greenpeace "rainbow warriors" ... on television, the audience may think that effective action has already taken place' (Rucht, 1993).

Specialist correspondents have become close to, and in part dependent for stories upon, leading pressure groups in the area they cover. Peter Riddell notes that from the late 1960s until at least the mid-1980s, most writers on social security were sympathetic to the views of the Child Poverty Action Group and similar bodies. There are plenty of excuses, notes William Waldegrave:

> *If you are producing a daily broadcast or daily newspaper always in a rush, a well organised group, who do most of the work for you, must seem like manna from heaven (Waldegrave, 1996).*

As Peter Bazalgette (1996) puts it:

> *We are now spoon-fed our stories, neatly packaged with 'evidence' and extreme conclusions, and all we have to do is pass the press release on to our readers, listeners or viewers. It's a cushy number, isn't it? ... you supply me with the extreme headline I need, ready written, and I'll be in the pub by opening time.*

PRESSURE GROUPS AND THE JUDICIARY

Pressure groups make more use of the courts in the USA than they do in Britain. In the USA, the law in relation to liability has fed the growth of special-interest lobbies.

However, pressure groups in Britain make more use of the courts than they did. Legal action is increasingly being used by environmental groups to win over public and business. For example, judicial review applications are used to challenge the granting of permits or licences to energy companies. Opponents of OPs have put increasing emphasis on action in the courts. Trade unions have taken up complaints from members about adverse health effects, pursuing cases of individual redress (see Appendix 4).

A key issue which forced the Conservative government to shelve its 1986 proposals to privatise the water industry was the legal controversy raised by the Council for the Protection of Rural England (CPRE) and the Institute for European Environmental Policy (IEEP) over the question of whether the Water Service Public Limited Companies would constitute 'competent authorities' under European law. Nigel Haigh, Director of the IEEP, had written to *The Times* on 13 May 1986, questioning whether the privatised water companies would constitute such 'competent authorities' (Richardson, Maloney and Rudig, 1992).

PRESSURE GROUPS AND LOCAL GOVERNMENT

According to Stoker (1991), most local authorities operate in the context of a world of active local pressure groups. Newton (1976) identified some 4,264 local organisations in his study of Birmingham. Many of these pressure groups are seeking to promote rather narrow interests, so that 'sporadic interventionism' assumes a 'highly individual and unorganised form with affected people arguing against one another for personal compensation and benefit' (Dowse and Hughes, 1977).

THE GROWTH OF PRESSURE-GROUP ACTIVITY AT THE LOCAL LEVEL

The opening-out of local authorities
Stoker shows how at least from the mid-1970s onwards many local authorities have 'opened out', creating new, if limited, opportunities for participation from a wider range of pressure groups, including cause groups.

The strengthening of local pressure-group politics
Matching the opening-out of local authorities, there has been a strengthening and a widening of the base of local pressure-group activity. Stoker (1991) singles out three elements in this process:

1 *The increased assertiveness and diversity of political activity.* Gyford identifies the general shift towards assertiveness and diversity among local groups in his research for the Committee of Inquiry into the Conduct of Local Authority Business, 1986.

> *The increasing need for local politicians to operate in a more open and responsive fashion can be seen as a direct reflection of social trends which are leading away from a rather quiescent and largely homogenous mass society towards one that is both more assertive and diversified.*

From the mid-1960s onwards, a fundamental shift in British political culture occurred, with traditional respect for and deference to public bodies and authorities being challenged by more questioning, sceptical and assertive attitudes.

Accompanying the increased assertiveness has been an increased diversity in the range of pressure groups that have mobilised. There has been

> *a proliferation of pressure groups at both local and national level, devoted to the achievement of quite particularised goals in such areas as pollution and the environment, sexual behaviour, media policy, animal welfare, homelessness, transport policy, energy policy and disarmament and defence*
>
> *Gyford, 1986.*

2 *An increased availability of resources to support this activity.*
3 *An increased willingness on the part of pressure groups and local authorities to share responsibility for service delivery.* It is groups from the voluntary sector that are to the fore in this activity. For a whole range of reasons, many local authorities have sought to use voluntary-sector agencies to provide services rather than providing these directly themselves. Given the rise of self-help organisations within the sector and a more general willingness to engage in campaigning activity, the potential for and likely effectiveness of voluntary-sector lobbying of local authorities has also been considerably enhanced.

The diversity and complexity of local pressure-group politics

The pattern of local authority pressure-group relationships is one of uneven development and diversity. Some authorities are more open than others, some have a more active group-base to deal with, and the nature of participating groups varies.

Local authorities are in an environment in which a range of non-elected agencies, voluntary organisations and other community-based groups can increasingly challenge their local dominance.

Stoker (1991) identifies three strategies that may be used by local authorities to manage their relationship with their increasingly complex and fragmented environment:

1 *arm's-length management*: setting up a Community Trust to administer and allocate funding to voluntary sector and community groups.
2 *sponsorship*: funding voluntary or community groups to monitor or oversee the performance of the non-elected agencies that have become key elements in a more fragmented local government system.
3 *encapsulation*: promoting a number of coordinating, cross-cutting representative forums as counters to the increasingly fragmented local decision-making environment.

SUMMARY

Pressure groups concentrate their activities where the power lies, and in the British system of government it traditionally lies in the executive.

The rise of the professional lobbyist has been a cause for concern, leading to the proposal for a Register of Lobbyists.

The growth of parliamentary lobbying has also been a cause for concern, leading to calls for greater control over lobbying.

Pressure groups have increasingly concentrated their activities upon the EU.

There are also circumstances in which pressure groups exert pressure through political parties, the mass media, the judiciary and local government.

STUDY GUIDES

Revision Hints

You should have knowledge of the relationships of pressure groups with other institutions.

Be able to answer the extent to which the rise of the professional lobbyist is a cause for concern, and whether there should be a Register of Lobbyists.

You should be able to explain the growth of parliamentary lobbying, and to assess both the extent to which it is a cause for concern and whether there should be greater control over lobbying.

Know the extent of, and be able to explain, the expansion of European lobbying.

Exam Hints

Answering essay questions on 'How Pressure Groups Operate'

1 a   Why is Parliament subjected to so much lobbying by pressure groups?
   b   Should there be greater control over lobbying?

Do not ignore the question set and write all you know about pressure groups. Focus on Parliament, and display knowledge about the work of parliamentary consultants. Explore the need for controls, and comment upon the problems of self-regulation.

2   A survey of pressure-group activities, conducted in 1990, produced the following conclusions:

The considerable increase in contact with European Community institutions, such as the European Parliament, was particularly evident. Almost two-thirds of groups reported an increase in contact with Europe. This increase was particularly marked in the responses of business and labour groups. Business groups were more likely to have established a European Office or joined a European-wide organisation.

(Adapted from R. Baggott, Talking Politics, Vol. 5 No. 1, p.21.)

To what extent and for what reasons has the attention of pressure groups moved away from Whitehall and Westminster to Brussels, Luxembourg and Strasbourg? (The Associated Examining Board Government and Politics Advanced Level Specimen Papers and Mark Schemes for Exams from 1997.)

Develop your answer to show the increasing relative importance of 'lobbying' at EU institution level, with use of examples. Mention the implications of the single market for different types of groups, as well as the differing networks which involve the 'power centres' of the EU.

1 Explain the shift in the attitude of the trade unions towards Europe in recent years.
2 How can cause groups influence governments?

5

THE EFFECTIVENESS OF PRESSURE GROUPS

Introduction

THIS CHAPTER WILL look at the capacity of pressure groups to influence government policy.

It will identify a number of factors which affect the capacity of pressure groups to influence government decisions. These are the resources of pressure groups, including size and quality of membership, income, the number and organisation of full-time staff; their access to government; their sanctions; and the economic and political circumstances in which they operate.

Key Points
- Resources
- Access
- Sanctions
- Economic and political circumstances.

RESOURCES

SIZE AND QUALITY OF MEMBERSHIP

A necessary, if not a sufficient, condition of effectiveness is having a large membership base (Grant, 1995b). The size of the membership base shows government that the pressure group has wide public support. For example, the

TUC is still Britain's largest pressure group. Its membership is impressive as compared to other European countries. The CBI has in its membership most large manufacturing companies. Environmental pressure groups have been very successful in the large increase in their membership (see Table 1 on p. 7).

However, as we saw in Chapter 2, modern large-scale cause groups are the product of mail-order marketing. They also have a large number of lapsed members. For example, only 35 per cent of those who joined FoE in 1991 rejoined in 1992 (Jordan and Maloney, 1997).

The quality of a pressure group's membership is perhaps more important than its quantity. In any large pressure group, most of the work in developing policy is done in committees. The central policy-making body of the TUC in the period between its annual conferences is the General Council, which is dominated by the leaders of the largest trade unions. This ensures that the quality of the General Council is high, and means that decisions taken by the Council have more chance of being accepted by the largest individual unions.

The decisions taken by the CBI's member firms, particularly on investment policy, have a crucial effect on the performance of the economy and are therefore likely to have a direct influence on the success of any given government, and, hence, on its chance of re-election.

Cause groups in Britain tend to attract a disproportionate number of well-educated, middle-class members. Jordan and Maloney shows that 35.3 per cent of FoE members had a first degree and 18.9 per cent a postgraduate degree, and that 10 per cent were still in higher education, making a total of 64 per cent of members with a high level of education.

However, any large pressure group is likely to be a more or less strong federation of divergent interests. For example, the TUC cannot ensure that the leadership of individual unions acts upon decisions of the General Council. At the same time, the individual union leadership cannot be sure that its membership will act upon its instructions. All this uncertainty weakens the bargaining position of the TUC in relation to government. The TUC is not a cohesive, monolithic organisation whose member unions share totally common attitudes and policy preferences. At any given time, the TUC may be more or less able to persuade its members that a particular policy line is advantageous. It cannot guarantee compliance.

The CBI suffers from what Grant (1993b) calls 'stifling breadth'. When he interviewed firms for the study of the CBI with Marsh in the mid-1970s, a number of firms, especially large firms, indicated that the CBI embraced too broad a spectrum of interests to be an authentic representative of their own particular interests. It had to make too many compromises to enable it to be a forceful critic of government policies. This criticism of stifling breadth re-emerged when Grant interviewed large firms for his work on government-relations divisions in the early 1980s. For example, a respondent in one major company commented: 'CBI is pretty useless, too broad a range of members to reach any worthwhile views.' Another company commented:

> *Our relations with CBI are friendly, but we're not very active. … CBI has to represent a range of companies. As an oil industry and American international company, we have special interests that may not align with those of the CBI*
>
> Grant, 1993.

Environmental pressure groups have been split by their objectives and methods. Objectives range from broad-based ecological concerns, for example Greenpeace, to the protection of a particular species, for example the RSPB. Methods range from traditional 'insider' tactics, that is informed and expert lobbying seeking to persuade politicians and civil servants of the case, to illegal forms of direct action. Environmental groups are also divided about objectives and methods at the European level. For example, the European Environmental Bureau (EEB) has a varied range of members, and this makes it difficult to coordinate their views effectively. While the EEB is a recognised and established part of the lobbying scene in Brussels, its effectiveness is, in practice, limited. Some of the greatest successes have been achieved by pressure groups with narrow and clearly defined objective. For example, the RSPB was closely involved with the European Commission in the formation of the EC Directive on the Conservation of Wild Birds (Garner, 1993).

The intensity of feeling among the pressure group's membership can be a key factor. A numerically small but intense group can often exert more influence than a large, less committed one. For example, the Shops Bill case showed how it is possible to block or delay decisions, even when a majority of the public is in favour of a change (see Appendix 2). Small, intense groups are often active at a local level, attempting to prevent development which they believe affects their community in an adverse way, for example Not In My Back Yard (NIMBY) groups.

INCOME

A large membership base provides income. However, the level of the financial resources of the TUC is more accurately seen as a weakness than as a strength. Many of its European equivalents, all smaller, are relatively better off. The income of the CBI is also small compared with its European equivalents.

The Countryside Alliance, which on 1 March 1998 organised the protest march in London against the banning of fox hunts, foreshadowed by the lighting of 5,500 beacons across the country, all under the slogan 'Let the Country Voice be heard', was financially guaranteed by the Duke of Westminster through a £1.3 million loan.

STAFF

Income enables the pressure groups to employ professional staff who can lobby decision-makers. The staff of the TUC are often skilled and knowledgeable. Some of the documents produced by the TUC, notably the annual *Economics Review*, are of a high standard. However, the staff is not really large enough to perform the wide range of tasks with which they are involved. Marsh (1983) found that one TUC official might be responsible for an area of policy which was the concern of between 10 and 20 senior civil servants. Inevitably, the civil servants were almost always better prepared.

Grant and Marsh (1977) found that the standard of the CBI's staff was often surprisingly high considering that it could not offer salaries, except at the top, which were likely to attract top-quality recruits from industry or government service. One of the strengths of the CBI has always been its ability to produce detailed, well-thought-out critiques of every aspect of government policy that has any relevance to the problems of business. Some of its publications, notably the *Industrial Trends Survey*, are widely accepted as authoritative contributions to ongoing debates on economic policy. However, one CBI staff member was responsible for a number of policy areas dealt with by several high-ranking staff in government. For example, one member of the CBI's Overseas Directorate was listed as being responsible for 'Non-Communist Asia east of Afghanistan including Japan'.

Lowe and Goyder's (1983) study of environmental groups found that around a fifth had no permanent staff at all, and over a half employed fewer than five people. At the European level, the EEB had three to four full-time staff members in 1992. 'Most of the approximately 15 EEB working groups meet only once a year' (Rucht, 1993). By contrast, the Conseil des Fédérations de l'Industrie Chimique, or European Council of Chemical Manufacturers Federation (CEFIC) alone had a staff of 80 and 4,000 company representatives involved in its committee work.

ORGANISATION

The Snowdrop campaign showed the almost inevitable need for organisation in successful protest. Starting as an apolitical, anonymous, unprofessional and amateur grouping, Snowdrop built itself a public profile with a competent leader (see Appendix 5).

Good organisation was crucial to both of the Druridge Bay campaigns (see Appendix 6). The initial pressure group, the Druridge Bay Association, mobilised local opinion on the nuclear issue. It was successful in generating media interest and promoting local authority opposition to the plans. However, it failed to draw together other interests opposed to nuclear power in such a way that resources could be maximised.

Residents, trade unions, local authorities, civic societies and conservation and environmental groups all had their own perspective on the issue. For example, the trade unions were mainly concerned about the impact on the coal industry, while the conservationists were concerned about harm to the local environment. Some campaigners were mutually suspicious of each other, particularly the anti-nuclear groups and the trade unions on the left against the middle-class conservation and civic groups behind the Centre-Right of the political spectrum. As the threat to the Bay loomed larger, a federation emerged in the form of the Druridge Bay Campaign. Care was taken to ensure that all perspectives were represented on its executive committee, with seats for trade unions, political parties, local authorities and environmental and civil groups. This strengthened the campaign. Once established, the Druridge Bay Campaign began to coordinate opposition far more effectively than the Druridge Bay Association had been able to.

The crucial factor in the defeat of the Shops Bill was the pressure exerted on MPs by a campaign at once both resolute and highly skilful. The various actors in the opposition were directed in a well-run, professional campaign, in contrast to the lacklustre and initially complacent 1986 campaign waged by the Bill's supporters, largely a matter of too little too late (see Appendix 2).

In 1993, the campaign group Keep Sunday Special (see Appendix 2) fought hard, and with costly professional backing, but this time they were unable to repeat their success in building up a head of steam against reform. By contrast, a strong and very effective campaign was fought by the Shopping Hours Reform Council. Unlike in the above-mentioned 1986 campaign, the retailers played a major part in the Council campaign, mainly through their own stores (see again Appendix 2).

ACCESS

Before any pressure group can have influence over government policy, it must normally have access to the decision-making process.

The crucial role which many of the CBI's member firms play in the economy ensures that the CBI has a level of access to the government decision-making process which few pressure groups can equal. Decisions taken by key industrialists about investment, expansion and employment are likely to be of major importance in determining the state of the economy. They influence the fate of a government, and such decisions are taken in the light of the government's performance in relation to industry. Administration in the industrial sphere intimately concerns the membership of the CBI and the various trade associations. This fact tends to ensure that these organisations have access to government. In addition, Grant and Marsh (1977) found that the CBI's contacts with ministers and civil servants were aided by the fact that senior CBI officials and committee chairmen shared educational backgrounds with them, an advantage which the TUC did not enjoy (see Table 16).

Table 16: *An analysis of the educational background of various elite groups*				
GROUPS	% WITH PUBLIC-SCHOOL EDUCATION	% FROM TOP PUBLIC SCHOOLS	% WITH OXBRIDGE EDUCATION	% WITH UNIVERSITY EDUCATION
Labour Cabinet Ministers 1970	29%	14%	52%	86%
Labour government ministers 1970	24%	8%	32%	64%
Conservative Cabinet ministers 1970	78%	55%	83%	83%
Conservative government ministers 1970	85%	53%	69%	79%
Senior civil servants 1974	69%	16%	84%	94%
Directors of top city institutions	82%	56%	59%	63%
Directors of leading companies	66%	23%	13%	53%
CBI Committee Chairmen 1965–73	78%	15%	41%	73%
TUC General Council 1955–75	0%	0%	13%	4%

SOURCE: GRANT AND MARSH, 1977.

Whitely and Winyard (1987) distinguish between promotional groups 'that speak on behalf of, or *for* the poor' and representational groups 'whose membership is made up *of* the poor, or a particular category of claimant'. They found that generally the promotional groups were more effective than the representational groups. This appeared to be because the representational groups were not seen by civil servants as truly representative of their categories, or able to deliver their clientele to civil servants, while the promotional groups displayed more professional expertise in pressure-group activity.

Media support is very important to the successful outcome of public campaigns by pressure groups. The role played by the mass media, in particular the press, was a vital factor in the Snowdrop campaign for tighter gun controls (see Appendix 5). The mass media played an extremely important role in mobilising public support behind both of the Druridge Bay campaigns (see Appendix 6). Central to understanding why the Brent Spa campaign was so successful is the relationship between Greenpeace and the media. Greenpeace successfully used the media to mobilise public opinion and force a major transnational corporation to make a complete 180-degree U-turn despite having full support from the British government (see Appendix 7).

SANCTIONS

NON-COOPERATION WITH THE ADMINISTRATION

The main sanction which most pressure groups have is non-cooperation with government in the consultation process which leads to legislation, and more especially in the administration of such legislation. The cost of administering legislation is high and becomes even higher if there is no cooperation forthcoming from the people or organisations to whom the legislation is to be applied.

For example, this was the tactic used by the vast majority of trade unions during the period 1971–74, when the 1971 Industrial Relations Act was rendered almost totally ineffective (see Appendix 1). The non-payment campaign promoted by the Anti-Poll Tax Federation was one of a number of factors behind its subsequent abolition (see Appendix 8). The teachers' unions' boycott of assessment tests in 1993 forced the government to undertake a review.

STRIKING, OR THE THREAT OF STRIKING

Obviously, some trade unions particularly are in key strategic positions within the economy, and as such can put pressure on employers and indirectly on government economic policy. For example, the NUM strike in 1974 succeeded when the then Conservative Prime Minister Edward Heath called an election which the Conservative Party lost (see Appendix 1).

The City of London can engage in a 'gilt-edged strike' by refusing to buy government stock, or talk down sterling because of unease about government policy.

The CBI has no very effective sanction on government. It could refuse to cooperate in the administration of any particular piece of legislation, but such a sanction depends on the cooperation of the individual firms directly involved. Such firms are likely to be reluctant to damage their own position with government by withdrawing cooperation. The CBI might also recommend that its members attempt to influence the economy by withholding investment as a threat to government. This is even less likely to be successful. Investment decisions by companies are not taken at the behest of the CBI. For example, although throughout 1972 and 1973, the CBI was issuing glowing commentaries on the economy and urging industrialists to invest, its exhortations had little direct effect on investment patterns. Neither the CBI nor individual manufacturing firms have a direct sanction equivalent to the strike or to the City's ability to move capital out of the country.

ECONOMIC AND POLITICAL CIRCUMSTANCES

ECONOMIC CIRCUMSTANCES

Economic circumstances, especially in relation to public expenditure, have an impact on the government's willingness to meet the demands of pressure groups. Against a background of continued pressure on public expenditure, changes in policy requiring more expenditure are unlikely to be met.

POLITICAL CIRCUMSTANCES

The political party in office can make a considerable difference to the effectiveness of a pressure group.

The Thatcher government, 1979–92

The effectiveness of contacts as perceived by the TUC changed dramatically after 1979. Between 1976 and 1979, the success rate in terms of the government's agreeing to take the action advocated by the TUC varied between 40.5 per cent and 47.0 per cent. In the years from 1979 to 1984, it ranged between 4.5 per cent and 22.5 per cent (Mitchell, 1987). Poverty groups were also adversely affected by the political climate of the 1980s. According to Whitely and Winyard (1987), in the Thatcherite era of conviction politics, their influence was reduced 'by the ideological beliefs of that administration, and by the deteriorating economic climate that monetarist policies' had created.

Other pressure groups perceived an improvement in their relationships with the government during the 1980s. This was either because they supported the ideas and policies of the Thatcher government, or because they could assist their development in some way. They included business organisations, rightwing think-tanks and conservative moral groups.

During the 1980s, a number of business organisations entered into a closer relationship with the government as advisers and consultants on the implementation of policies. For example, the advertising industry and the financial sector were able to exert considerable influence over the details of the government's privatisation programme through their expertise. This was illustrated by the withdrawal of nuclear power from the electricity privatisation plans in 1989, a reversal in policy promoted by the government's own advisers. However, the influence of consultancy firms such as solicitors, accountants, merchant bankers and management consultants was not confined to the work for which they were paid. This gave them valuable experience and useful contacts for lobbying on issues affecting their own interests.

Other private-sector lobbies also found themselves drawn close to the government as a result of policies which sought to increase their role in the delivery of public services. These included the public schools, private health providers and companies tendering for public-sector contracts.

Not all business organisations enjoyed a cordial relationship with the government, however. The CBI had a difficult relationship with the government in the Thatcher era. For some ministers, particularly those on the right of the Conservative Party, the CBI was tainted by its involvement with the corporatist politics of the 1970s (see Chapter 3). They preferred the more 'New Right' spirit of the Institute of Directors, which improved its relationship with government during the 1980s, as did the Association of British Chambers of Commerce and other groups specifically representing small businesses.

The Thatcher government was also more receptive than previous governments to the views of rightwing ideological groups. During the 1980s, these enjoyed greater access to ministers and exerted considerable influence over policy. Rightwing think-tanks such as the Centre for Policy Studies, the Adam Smith Institute and the Institute for Economic Affairs became a rich source of ideas for the government, playing a key role in health and education reforms, as well as in the field of privatisation and contracting out.

During the 1980s, the government was also more open than its predecessors to lobbying from conservative moral groups such as the Conservative Family Campaign and the National Viewers' and Listeners' Association. A number of reforms illustrated their growing influence, for example the establishment of the Broadcasting Standards Council, restrictions on video recordings, new controls on sex education, and an amendment to the 1989 Local Government Act which outlawed the promotion of homosexuality by local authorities.

Local campaigns
Local campaigns can benefit from favourable political circumstances.

The Druridge Bay campaigns (see Appendix 6)
The Druridge Bay campaigns drew strength from a national shift in public opinion, forming part of a groundswell of concern which forced environmental and nuclear-power issues onto the political agenda in the 1980s and early 1990s.

The political climate can assist some local groups more than others. No matter how favourable the political climate, some schemes cannot be halted by protest, too much political and financial capital having been invested in them, making abandonment virtually impossible. Others, nearer the drawing-board stage, can more easily gain a reprieve. For example, Druridge Bay was on the shortlist for nuclear power but was fortunate in that Hinkley and Sizewell ranked above it.

Other circumstances certainly assisted the anti-nuclear campaign at Druridge. Accidents in the USA at Three Mile Island in 1979 and in Russia at Chernobyl in 1986 had a major impact on public attitudes towards nuclear power.

Another crucial factor was the Thatcher government's decision to privatise nuclear power. This gave protestors a fresh opportunity to mobilise public and parliamentary opinion. Furthermore, the privatisation plan exposed the industry's finances to the scrutiny of financial advisers, who declared it an unattractive investment for the private sector, largely because of the hidden costs associated with waste disposal and decommissioning. This forced a review of the industry and a moratorium on public-sector investment in new nuclear-power stations. As a *Guardian* journalist observed at the time, the woolly-pullovered environmentalists' staunchest ally turned out to be the sharp-suited city accountant.

Circumstances also played an important part in the sand-extraction campaign. Ready Mixed Concrete and Northern Aggregates were seeking to develop other sites in the region, and it is possible that Druridge was a useful card to play in negotiations with the local planning authority. It was by no means certain that the Druridge site would have remained an economic proposition in the future, and it was therefore possible that extraction could have ceased anyway before planning permission expired.

Another point regarding circumstances is that the sand-extraction campaign undoubtedly benefited from the previous campaign against nuclear power. Although the sand issue attracted public concern in its own right, it is doubtful that on its own it would have had the same resonance. The second campaign rode on the back of the first, drawing on the level of public support already built up and benefiting from its effective organisation and political networks.

The Snowdrop campaign (see Appendix 5)
Events in 1996 and 1997 gave credence to the aims of Snowdrop. The Port Arthur massacre in Australia, which also involved guns, brought the events in Dunblane back into the minds of the public, and the Australian government's swift implementation of comprehensive gun-control measures compared favourably with the perceived inaction of the British government. A further school attack, this time with a machete, at St. Luke's School in Wolverhampton, raised the issues of security and weapon restrictions.

ASSESSMENT OF EFFECTIVENESS

The effectiveness of pressure groups is difficult to assess.

According to Toke (1996), environmental groups can be effective in two ways:

1 by influencing policy details, as exemplified by the 'open' strategy that led to amendments to the 1995 Environment Act (see p. 10).

2 by shifting the policy agenda through overtly outsider campaigning tactics such as those which preceded the cutbacks in the road-building programme.

However, just because a particular policy change happens to correspond with pressure-group demands does not necessarily mean that it was the activities of the pressure groups that led to the change in policy. For example, the cuts in the Conservative government's road-building plans, announced in 1994, might seem to represent a government response to increasing public concern about road-building plans, reflected in the activities of environmental groups. Or they could be seen as a recognition by the government that building more roads does not cut congestion in the long run because it encourages more trips to be made. The latter points to the potential influence of an 'informed debate about the limitations of existing policy' (Grant, 1995a).

SUMMARY

The factors which affect the capacity of pressure groups to influence government policy are their resources, including size and quality of membership, income, the number and organisation of full-time staff; their access to government; their sanctions; and the economic and political environment in which they operate.

STUDY GUIDES

Make sure you know the factors which affect the capacity of pressure groups to influence government decisions.

Answering essay questions on 'The Effectiveness of Pressure Groups'

1 Why are some pressure groups more successful than others?

> Identify key factors such as resources, including size and quality of membership, income, and the number and organisation of full-time staff. However, do not simply write a list of factors but explain why some pressure groups are more successful than others, even though they might have, for example, fewer members. Offer examples of pressure groups to illustrate the points you wish to make. Consider what actually constitutes success.

2 'The key to the effectiveness of a pressure group is to have a large membership base.' Discuss.

> The key to this question is first to define what makes a pressure group effective, and then second to sustain or oppose the point that a large membership is the key element.

1 How have the factors determining the ability of pressure groups to influence policy changed in recent years?
2 'It is incorrect to say that outsider environmental pressure is necessarily an inferior way of influencing government compared to insider tactics' (Toke, 1996). Discuss.

6

PRESSURE GROUPS, DEMOCRACY AND EFFECTIVE GOVERNMENT

Introduction

THIS CHAPTER WILL look at ways in which pressure groups can both help and hinder democracy. It will also look at the extent to which pressure groups promote effective government.

Key Points
- Pressure groups and democracy
- Pressure groups and effective government.

PRESSURE GROUPS AND DEMOCRACY

HELP TO DEMOCRACY

A channel of representation
In pluralist theory, pressure-group activity is seen as an intrinsic part of democracy. Bentley (1908) may have overstated his case when he argued that individuals cannot affect governments except through pressure groups (see pp. 5–6). However, according to McKenzie (1958):

---

pressure groups, taken together, are a far more important channel of communication than parties for the transmission of political ideas from the mass of the citizenry to their rulers.

As we saw in Chapter 2, when most citizens attempt to influence the decision-making process of their elected representatives, they do so through pressure groups.

A means of political participation

As Des Wilson, one of Britain's most experienced and successful lobbyists, argues:

> *there is more to democracy than the occasional vote. To be healthy, a democracy needs participation at every level. Pressure groups are the one way by which people can exercise their right to know and to comment on what is happening, and to argue for different policies and priorities throughout a government's term of office*
>
> *Wilson, 1984.*

Moreover, by participating in pressure-group activity, people may become more willing to participate in the political process generally. There is evidence that pressure groups play an important role both in encouraging people to participate in a range of political activities and in providing resources to enable them to get involved (Parry, Moyser and Day, 1992).

William Waldegrave, Chief Secretary to the Treasury, said in 1996 that pressure groups are a natural part of politics. People will always group together to protect their interests, to argue for change, or to oppose change in a system where things can be changed by political action. 'The more democratic the system is', he added, 'the more such groups are likely to flourish' (Waldegrave, 1996).

A check on excessive government power

By representing a broad range of interests and preferences in society, and by mobilising public opinion, pressure groups can check the concentration of political power. They may do this by generating opposition to government policies formulated without regard to the views of the general public or to the interests of a significant minority likely to be affected. Alternatively, if pressure groups are recognised by government, they may exert influence through consultation before policy is finally decided, a procedure clearly in line with the principle of government by consent.

HINDRANCE TO DEMOCRACY

Special interests

As we saw in Chapter 2, political parties aggregate the mass of interests in society, without which politics would be dominated by special interests. The relative importance of pressure groups has increased in recent years.

Fears of academic theorists like Olson (1965), that the logic of collective action could lead to the tyrannising of the majority by minority interests (see pp. 16–17), and Brittan (1975), that the pursuit of group self-interest through coercive means in the marketplace was a serious threat to democracy (see p. 17), have not been confined to the New Right.

Douglas Hurd, a non-Thatcherite Conservative minister, said, in a speech to the annual conference of the Royal Institute of Public Administration in 1986, that the weight of pressure groups had very substantially increased in recent years and added greatly to the difficulties of achieving decisions in the general interest. They were like 'serpents constantly emerging from the sea to strangle Laocoon and his sons in their coils' (his reference was to Laocoon, a priest in Greek legend who warned the Trojans against the wooden horse).

William Waldegrave, another non-Thatcherite Conservative minister, said about 10 years later that Parliament

> *should be wary of responding to the demands of lobby groups unless they are sure that in doing so they are improving the health of the body politic as a whole.*

The clearest conflicts, but not the only conflicts, he added, arose over money. Many pressure groups – industrial, charitable, ephemeral or long-established – exist to persuade the government to spend more on their favourite subject. Waldegrave said that, as Andrew Cooper's analysis of the *Today* programme, *Costing the Public Policy Agenda: a Week of the Programme*, showed, 'by far the most regular demand of anybody campaigning for anything is for taxpayers' (now also lottery players') cash'. He added that, as Olson argued, in any one case 'the spending consequence may be small for the population as a whole, but the benefit very great for the lobby group or its clients'. The government saying 'yes' too often was the principal reason why the dynamic of public spending in most democratic countries was ever upwards, which has 'grave consequences for the population as a whole'. He concluded that 'there is a duty to the common good as well as the particular' (Waldegrave, 1996).

Jimmy Carter, in his farewell address as Democrat President of the USA to the nation, put the single-issue and special-interest pressure groups in the frame as the cause of his government's problems:

> *We are increasingly drawn to single-issue groups and special interest organisations to insure that whatever else happens our personal views and our own private interests are protected. ... This tends to distort our purpose because the national interest is not always the sum of all our single or special interests.*

A lack of internal democracy

According to the elitist Michels, the iron law of oligarchy means that it is in the nature of organisations for power to be concentrated in the hands of a small group of dominant figures. Pressure groups seem just as affected by Michels' iron law of oligarchy as are political parties. Many cause groups deliberately avoid democratic structures. In some cases, such as Greenpeace, they are 'not even remotely democratic bodies' (Riddell, 1996). Internally, Greenpeace has:

> ... *a strictly bureaucratic, if not authoritarian, structure. A small group of people has control over the organisation both at the international level and within national chapters. Local action groups, which exist in some countries, are totally dependent on the central body and the rank and file is excluded from all decisions*
>
> *Rucht, 1993.*

Such pressure groups are more like supporters clubs: 'Major British organizations such as the RSPB, FoE, and Amnesty, are best seen as organizations with financial supporters rather than membership bodies' (Jordan and Maloney, 1997).

In other cases, high membership figures, such as the over two million who belong to the National Trust, are more to do with the associated benefits of membership, such as being able to visit historic buildings or monuments, than with a particular view about the heritage or the environment (Riddell, 1996).

THE HIGH MEMBERSHIP FIGURES OF THE NATIONAL TRUST, A LEADING UK ENVIRONMENTAL PRESSURE GROUP, ARE ACHIEVED BY THE BENEFITS OF MEMBERSHIP, WHICH INCLUDE BEING ABLE TO VISIT HISTORIC BUILDINGS OR MONUMENTS

The larger sectional groups, such as the TUC and the CBI, tend to have formal democratic structures, but they are oligarchic in practice.

Even in the case of some professional bodies, with a very high percentage of those qualified to belong, it is no longer true that the official spokespersons of elected officials speak for all members, as the divisions in the Law Society have shown (Riddell, 1996).

Parry, Moyser and Day (1992) define participation in terms not of 'mere membership' of organisations but of being 'based on actions, on doing things which are intended to have some effect on political outcomes'. Jordan and Maloney see the political significance of mass cause-group membership as marginal because the costs of such participation are so low that it cannot be assumed that members are making the commitment and investment implied by participation. There cannot be confidence that participation to the limited extent that is found in mail-order groups (see p. 9) is a significant democratic form of activity. On the other hand, these protest businesses do not naïvely lead and hope that members will follow. As sensible businesses, they have done their market research, for example through membership surveys, and know what members can 'live with'. The 'role of such anticipated reaction' can therefore be powerful in maintaining a link, however tenuous, between the leadership elite and membership 'supporters'. However, this 'falls some way short of internal democracy' (Jordan and Maloney, 1997).

Many pressure groups offer what has been termed *astroturf* not *grass-roots* opportunities for participation (Cigler and Loomis, 1995). This is clearly demonstrated by the comment of one FoE organiser who said in an interview in 1995: 'Members have to decide to back us or not. We make policy and if they don't like it they can join some other group' (Jordan and Maloney, 1997). Decision-making in most pressure groups can be termed at best as anticipatory rather than participatory democracy, more critically as anticipatory oligarchy. Decisions are made by the few on behalf of the mass within a framework which the few believe will be popular enough to maintain support.

Political inequality

Elitism, which sees power as concentrated in the hands of a few, argues that pressure-group activity tends to reinforce existing patterns of inequality in the political system.

For example, the shared educational backgrounds of senior CBI officials and committee chairpersons with ministers and senior civil servants, very different from the educational background of members of the General Council of the TUC (see Table 16 on p. 81), might explain why the CBI had better informal contacts with government departments than the TUC.

Membership of cause groups is skewed towards those with higher educational attainments. 35.3 per cent of FoE members and 26 per cent of Amnesty International members have degrees, compared to 8 per cent of the general population. 18.9 per cent and 26.5 per cent of FoE and Amnesty members respectively have a postgraduate degree (Jordan and Maloney, 1997).

PRESSURE GROUPS AND EFFECTIVE GOVERNMENT

HELP TO EFFECTIVE GOVERNMENT

Advice
Pressure groups improve government effectiveness by providing advice to government (see p. 31).

Consultation
Graham and Tytler (1993) observe in the context of education policies, 'partnerships and consultation do not lessen government power to govern, they can enhance its effectiveness'. The failure of the Conservative governments to consult the teaching profession, and other interested parties such as the local authorities, led to ineffective schemes which had to be modified later for practical reasons (see p. 82).

Assistance in administration
Pressure groups also help in the administration of government policy (see p. 31). For example, an employers' association may be able to assist in making a policy effective at the level of the firm by disseminating information about the policy and its applicability to its members. It may also explain its relevance to their particular needs through such mechanisms as seminars or contacts with individual firms.

A more active form of cooperation arises when an association assumes responsibility for a task that would otherwise have to be discharged by government. For example, an association may devise a self-regulating code of conduct in a particular problem area that obviates the need for direct government regulation.

Responsibility for what was formerly a public policy function may even be transferred to employer-led associations, as in the case of the Training and Enterprise Councils (TECs).

HINDRANCE TO EFFECTIVE GOVERNMENT

When pressure groups get it wrong
A pressure group is often assumed to be the definitive voice on a particular subject. However, there is a danger of taking claims at face value. Bazalgette,

producer of TV food programmes and the creator of BBC2's *Food and Drink*, warned of 'the mayhem caused when well-meaning pressure groups either exaggerate their case or simply get it wrong' (Bazalgette, 1996).

Poisoned apples
A US television documentary in the eighties argued that since children eat more apples than adults, the risk from Alar, the trade name of an apple spray Daminozide, was higher for them, and so it should be banned. Although some tests on rats had found no link between Alar and cancer, further tests found that, in massive quantities, it could cause cancer in mice but not hamsters or dogs. Alar was permitted for use by the Food and Drink Administration – the US government safety level at the time aimed at reducing the risk of cancer to one in a million.

Within days, the actress Meryl Streep was heading a pressure group dedicated to the banning of Alar. In Britain, the actress Pamela Stephenson founded the pressure group Parents for Safe Food, also to get Alar withdrawn, which it was. However, Meryl Streep changed her mind, in the end, because the proper approach to risk and scientific data was explained to her. One man in particular, Professor Bruce Ames of Stanford University, has insisted that the potency to animals of a substance must be set against frequency of consumption (Bazalgette, 1996).

Killer ketchup
Some years ago, a health alert was issued jointly by FoE and Parents for Safe Food. Tomato ketchup and brown bread had been found to contain alarmingly high levels of ETU (ethylene thiourea), a fungicide crop spray, linked with lung, liver and thyroid cancer, as well as birth defects.

When the Ministry of Agriculture carried out their own tests on the same foods shortly afterwards, they found much, much lower levels of residues which were within the safety limit then in force. It transpired that the laboratory that had carried out the analysis for the pressure groups had made an error. The high levels of ETU came from a rubber bung in a glass vessel which had contaminated the food samples (Bazalgette, 1996).

Radioactive food
The irradiation of food involves exposing it to gamma rays or X-rays. This can be used to inhibit the sprouting of potatoes, to kill insects in grains and spices, and to accelerate the ageing of freshly milled flour to make it suitable for breadmaking. In slightly higher doses, it can be used to kill food bacteria. It is a legalised process so long as the treated food is labelled as such. In Bazalgette's view, supermarkets have shunned it because at the time of its legislation a pressure group was set up to oppose it. This coincided with the Chernobyl accident, and as a consequence, the campaign was operating on fertile ground.

Arguments against irradiated food included that not enough was known about its long-term effects, it affected the nutritional value of food detrimentally, and it could be used to reduce bacteria in food that would otherwise be unfit for consumption. In fact, contaminated prawns were treated in this way in Holland and resold. So clearly, its use needed to be controlled. However, the truth was that vitamin loss was comparable with other food processes such as canning or freezing, and it has long been used to sterilise food for astronauts and very sick hospital patients with no ill-effects whatsoever. It is just another industrial food process that needs to be used as carefully and responsibly as any other.

Beef madness
British beef was banned in Europe, by the open admission of EU commissioners, not because they believed it was unsafe but because it did not have 'consumer confidence'. This, according to Bazalgette, was 'the ultimate result of the pressure-group society we live in'.

Brent Spar
Greenpeace made a mistake leading to an over-estimate by the pressure group of the amount of oil contained within the installation (see Appendix 7).

Non-cooperation with the administration

If pressure groups refuse to cooperate with government in the consultation process which leads to legislation, and more especially in the administration of such legislation, the effects can be dramatic. For example, during the period 1971–74, the 1971 Industrial Relations Act was rendered almost totally ineffective by the non-cooperation of the vast majority of trade unions (see Appendix 1).

CONCLUSION

The danger of a corporatist arrangement, in which a few sectional groups are powerful, has been replaced by a post-industrial danger of a large number of cause groups promoting their causes. There may be an inability to take effective political decisions with this dispersal of power, which is as great a danger as the concentration of power under corporatism.

SUMMARY

Pressure groups are an additional channel of representation, necessary because a small number of political parties cannot possibly represent all interests within society. They act as a check upon the power of the government, keeping it responsive to the wishes of the population between elections.

However, pressure groups represent special interests. Their activity tends to reinforce existing concentrations of power.

Pressure groups improve government effectiveness by providing advice to government, and sometimes also by helping in the administration of government policy.

However, there are dangers when pressure groups either exaggerate their case or simply get it wrong. Pressure groups may also make administration difficult and costly if they fail to cooperate.

STUDY GUIDES

Revision Hints

Make sure you understand ways in which pressure groups can both help and hinder democracy.

You should also be able to explain the extent to which pressure groups promote effective government.

Exam Hints

Answering essay questions on 'Pressure Groups, Democracy and Effective Government'

1 Do pressure groups help or hinder democracy?
   Make reference to theories of pluralism and democracy. Give a rigorous examination of the practical operation of pressure groups. Examine alternative perspectives and theories in order to give structure to your work.
2 Do pressure groups prevent effective government?
   Do not write about the effectiveness of pressure groups, and be sure of what makes a government an effective one. You should analyse hindrances to effective government from certain pressure groups. However, you should also note the need for advice and assistance for effective government, and that pressure groups provide such advice and assistance.

Practice Questions

1 'The main problem with pressure groups in Britain is how to relate them to the public interest.' Discuss.
2 Discuss the view that pressure groups make Britain harder to govern.

APPENDICES: CASE STUDIES

APPENDIX 1   TRADE UNIONS IN THE 1970s

TRADE UNIONS AND THE CONSERVATIVE GOVERNMENT 1970–74

The trade unions and industrial relations policy

THE CONSERVATIVE PARTY won the General Election in 1970 committed to introducing a bill to 'put unions on a legal footing', which had been a major plank in their election manifesto. The Industrial Relations Act was passed in 1971 which severely restricted the autonomy of trade unions and trade unionists.

Although the trade unions failed to amend the legislation, they effectively restricted its implementation. The TUC advised affiliated unions not to register under the Act and not to co-operate with the National Industrial Relations Court (NIRC), but to attend its proceedings only when an action was brought against them. This strategy proved so successful that by the end of 1972 the legislation was little used. The trade unions' opposition to the legislation was helped by the fact that large companies and employers' organisations did not use its provisions for fear of damaging relations with employees.

The trade unions and incomes policy

The Conservative government elected in 1970 was committed to a reduction of government intervention in the economy and therefore to a voluntary incomes policy. However, despite the introduction of tripartite, and later multipartite talks on a voluntary policy, the government continued to listen to economists, notably within the Treasury, advocating statutory controls. A statutory policy was introduced in 1972. One union, the NUM, refused to adhere to Stage Three of the incomes policy. Against the background of the oil crisis, and some inept political judgements, the miners succeeded in undermining the policy when Heath called a general election, which he lost.

THE SOCIAL CONTRACT

During this period of confrontation between the trade unions and the Conservative government, relations between the trade unions and the Labour

Party substantially improved. The trade unions sought and achieved a commitment from the Labour Party to repeal the 1971 Industrial Relations Act, and to enact certain legislation to improve the position of the employee within industry, in return for a commitment on incomes from the TUC.

TRADE UNIONS AND THE LABOUR GOVERNMENTS 1974–79

The trade unions and industrial relations policy

The minority Labour government passed the 1974 Trade Union and Labour Relations Act which repealed the 1971 Industrial Relations Act. Subsequently, the majority Labour government passed the 1975 Employment Protection Act which strengthened employees' rights in a wide variety of fields and in addition made it compulsory for employers to disclose to representatives of independent trade unions information which was necessary for collective bargaining purposes.

The trade unions and incomes policy

The Labour Party came back to office in 1974 committed to a voluntary incomes policy. Initially, the trade unions and the Labour Party entered into a loose agreement on wages policy. Subsequently, agreement was reached on three phases in 1975, 1976 and 1977, which proved successful in restricting wage levels before the policy collapsed in 1978.

CONCLUSION

The trade unions did enjoy significant negative power in the industrial relations field. Individual unions in strategic industries did exert considerable direct or indirect influence over government policy in the wages sphere. During the period of the Social Contract, the TUC almost for the first time had positive influence over policy, which lasted until 1975.

Source: Marsh, D. (ed) (1983) *Pressure Politics*, London: Junction Books

APPENDIX 2   SUNDAY SHOPPING

INTRODUCTION

The history of the regulation of Sunday trading goes back at least five centuries to the Fairs and Markets Act, 1448, but at the time of the 1986 Shops Bill, the relevant legislation was the Shops Act 1950. Part IV of that Act dealt with Sunday trading. Its provisions covered England and Wales, and stated that all shops must be closed for the serving of customers on a Sunday except for those listed in Schedule 5 in Part V of the Act. This made it illegal to sell fresh fruit and vegetables, confectionery and tobacco, medicines, newspapers, motor accessories and meals or refreshments on or off the premises. It was also illegal to sell antiques and furniture, electrical goods, cars, books, clothing, hardware and garden equipment, and fish and chips. One could thus buy a pornographic magazine (because it is a periodical) but not a bible (because it is a book). It was possible to buy fish from a fishmonger, but not meat from a butcher. One could not buy fish and chips, but take-away Chinese food was permissible (because, at the time the Act was passed, no-one could envisage the existence of Chinese food on a large scale, so fish and chips were mentioned explicitly in the Act rather than take-away food in general).

Because of the many anomalies it was found to contain, there were many attempts to reform the 1950 Shops Act in the 30 years following its passage. All these, with one exception, came in the form of private members' bills and made little significant progress in Parliament (the exception was a 1956 government bill which encountered substantial opposition in the House of Lords; when it came to the House of Commons, late in the session, the government chose not to proceed with it). Pressure for reform increased in the 1980s. Not only was the law coming to be seen as an anachronism but, with the growth of DIY stores and garden centres, which saw Sundays as one of their main days for trade, it was increasingly being ignored. Enforcement by the local authorities, whose responsibility it was, was sporadic. Significantly, a bill by Baroness Trumpington, then a Conservative backbencher in the House of Lords, which would have repealed all restrictions on Sunday trading, passed all its stages in the Lords in 1981 but failed to make any significant progress in the Commons. More important, two years earlier, a Conservative government with a strong free-market philosophy had been elected; and it was re-elected in 1983.

THE BACKGROUND TO THE SHOPS BILL AND ITS INTRODUCTION

Despite having the family background of a small grocer's shop (it is small shopkeepers who were said to be most at risk from unrestricted Sunday trading), Mrs Thatcher was known to be unhappy about the state of the Sunday trading laws. Not only was the law being widely flouted, and not only was it held by some to be in disrepute, but the Prime Minister also saw regulation as an unnecessary and undesirable restriction on the rights of shops to trade how and when they wanted. In this view, she received strong support from senior members of the government.

To them, the need for reform was obvious, and equally clearly the fate of 18 private members' bills since 1950 demonstrated that a successful attempt at change would have to come in the form of a government bill. However, the government was not sure how the law needed to be amended. To solve the problem, in August 1983, just two months after the 1983 General Election, Leon Brittan, the Home Secretary, set up a Committee of Inquiry

to consider what changes are needed in the Shops Acts, having regard to the interests of consumers, employers and employees and to the traditional character of Sunday, and to make recommendations as to how these should be achieved.

It was chaired by Robin Auld QC. The hope was that the Committee would produce an answer broadly in line with the government's philosophy. It took 14 months over its deliberations. It solicited public responses and took out advertisements in the national press asking members of the public to submit their views. More than 300 organisations and 7,000 individuals submitted written evidence, and 12 major bodies gave oral evidence.

The view that any partial form of deregulation was not practicable, together with the economic arguments, led the Committee to its overall conclusion published in November 1984: 'We recommend the abolition in England, Wales and Scotland of all legal restrictions on the hours for which shops may be open to server customers'. A motion to this effect was carried decisively in the House of Commons by 304 votes to 184, though 26 Conservative MPs voted with the opposition.

The government saw the issue of Sunday trading as a problem that needed to be solved once and for all, and considered that the way to do so was to introduce a bill to enact the recommendations of the Auld Committee and not to worry about partial solutions. Accordingly, the Queen's Speech at the start of the 1985–86 session stated that 'A Bill will be introduced to remove statutory restrictions on shop opening hours.' The Shops Bill, which abolished all restrictions on shop opening hours, was introduced in the House of Lords, where it had its second reading on 2 December 1985. This decision was on the face of it a strange one, especially when it is considered that some of those in Parliament potentially most opposed to Sunday trading, namely the bishops, are there. The ostensible reason, according to the Leader of the House of Commons, John Biffen, was the need to balance the flow of legislation between the two Houses and the desire to spread the legislative load for the Home Office. However, clearly there were other factors. First, the whips did not want a potentially controversial bill in the

Commons so early in the session, and second, Baroness Trumpington's bill had got through all its stages in the Lords, and it might be hoped that a repetition would provide some encouragement for the Commons (though it is arguable that part of the reason for that success was that the peers believed that it would make no progress in the Commons).

The decision to go first to the Lords appeared to be vindicated when the Bill had a smooth passage. Conservative backbenchers, free from constituency pressure, were prepared to vote for the Bill, and it went through its various stages at quite a rapid pace. It was finally passed without a division. However, the more difficult hurdle the Bill had to face was the Commons, and with hindsight, the decision to go to the Lords first was a mistake. The government had given its opponents time to mobilise their supporters both inside and outside Parliament.

THE CAMPAIGN FOR THE BILL

As the body representing consumers, the National Consumer Council (NCC) had long been in favour of a change in the law which would bring about total deregulation.

The belief that, once the government had decided to introduce legislation and could apply a whip, the issue was basically settled, was a common one among the Bill's supporters, and led to a sense of complacency. The NCC had an added structural problem. While the 'anti' campaign was able to get people to put pressure on their individual MPs, the NCC was essentially a centralised body dealing with government without a local structure, and so was unable to initiate a letter-writing campaign as the 'antis' did. It therefore ignored almost entirely a tactic that was used to great effect by opponents of the Bill. There were two other aspects of its campaign, both born of complacency, that the NCC later regretted. The first was the decision not to pay any attention to the opposition parties. It was assumed that all Labour MPs would vote against the Bill, and that the same would happen with the Alliance. Second, the NCC gave no thought to any of the possible compromises that were being suggested in the period leading up to the Commons debate on the second reading of the Bill.

The other major supporters of the Bill were several of the large retailers, who had come together in a loose coalition known as Open Shop. This came into being in 1982 after the failure, at second reading, of a private members' bill which had been introduced by Ray Whitney to liberalise Sunday trading. Open Shop consisted of the chairpersons of five major retailers: Woolworths, Asda, W.H. Smith, Harris Queensway and Habitat/Mothercare. However, it did not see itself as a campaigning organisation.

All the member organisations of Open Shop gave evidence to the Auld Committee, and once it had reported, Open Shop tried to persuade the government that its recommendations made sense. To do this, it concentrated on producing research from other countries which did permit Sunday trading. All this research was passed on to the government, and Open Shop appeared to have achieved its objective when the government announced that it was bringing forward a bill. Like the NCC, the retailers assumed that the battle had been won. Very little effort was made to pass on the research findings to individual MPs.

THE CAMPAIGN AGAINST THE BILL

Many groups that would not consider themselves usual allies fought together on this single issue. It is possible to distinguish two distinct parts, differentiated by reasons for opposing the Bill, and by whom they chose to try to influence. As the union representing shopworkers, the Union of Shop, Distributive and Allied Workers (USDAW) opposed deregulation, which it saw as detrimental to the interests of its members. However, USDAW was just one part of a larger coalition. The most important work in building up opposition at a local level was done by the religious bodies. Much of the work of coordinating the Churches' response to the Bill was undertaken by the Jubilee Centre, a Christian economic and social research institute founded in 1983. Through this Centre, the Pro-Sunday Coalition was formed. This gradually extended its membership beyond evangelicals, being transformed first into the Keep Sunday Special Coalition and then into the Keep Sunday Special Campaign. The Jubilee Centre played a leading part in the written campaign, producing a stream of well-researched leaflets and booklets against the Bill.

The massive organisational structure of the Churches and the total commitment of their local leaders – priests, ministers and lay preachers – to the Keep Sunday Special cause was a powerful weapon aimed at a single target. Sunday by Sunday, the faithful were exhorted to preserve the Lord's Day, which they were in the very act of celebrating. Petitions were at the back of the church or chapel to be signed, notices were displayed about public meetings, and from the pulpit and the altar came urgent pleas to write letters to the local MP and the Home Secretary.

Many thousands of people followed this advice. The Home Office alone received no fewer than 68,000 letters in the ratio of 2 to 1 against the Bill. This was the final figure; earlier correspondence in favour of the Bill had been negligible. In February 1986, in a written answer, David Waddington, a Home Office minister, had revealed that his department had received 25,282 letters against the Bill and only 58 in favour.

However, the extra-parliamentary campaign was not simply a matter of writing letters and presenting petitions. The Keep Sunday Special Coalition was transformed into the nationally based Keep Sunday Special Campaign, with well-known political and Church figures as patrons. The main thrust of the

Campaign's strategy was to bring pressure to bear on MPs at constituency level, while simultaneously organising parliamentary opposition to the Bill at Westminster. Thus, emphasis was placed on press publicity at local and regional level, together with substantial use of local radio, as well as detailed briefing of members of both Houses of Parliament.

THE DEBATE IN THE HOUSE OF COMMONS

The Shops Bill passed its third reading in the Lords on 25 February 1986. In the seven weeks that elapsed before the second reading in the Commons, there occurred a period of intense lobbying and tactical manoeuvring.

Having been largely inactive up to this point, the campaign in favour of the Bill now realised the scale of the opposition. In a written answer to Peter Bruinvels on 3 March 1986, the Prime Minister said that the government had received about 800 representations in favour of its proposals and about 40,000 against since the debate on the Auld Report in the House of Commons. Supporters of the Bill now started to mobilise. Large retailers told their customers to write in its favour. Clearly the strategy had considerable effect as the Prime Minister was able to say in a written reply to Bruinvels on 26 March 1986 that the government had received about 7,700 representations in favour of its proposals and about 45,000 representations against; by 15 April, the figures had become 20,736 for and 47,354 against. Several DIY stores and garden centres started petitions in support of Sunday trading, though of the 161 petitions presented before the House on the subject of Sunday trading, 158 were against the Bill.

The opponents of the Bill meanwhile continued their intensive campaign. An increasing number of Conservative MPs began to have doubts about it, and this was expressed in substantial support for two Early-Day Motions. The government imposed a three-line whip at second reading, but with the promise of free votes at the committee and report stages.

Whether the government might just have won the vote if the debate had gone well for the Bill, perhaps by fewer votes against and more abstentions on the Conservative side, is open to question, but from the government's point of view the debate was a disaster. In particular, the Home Secretary made a crucial error during the debate by pledging that at no stage would he seek to move a guillotine on the Bill, thus opening the way to talking the Bill out at a later stage. The waverers realised that, with no time limit, the committee stage of the Bill would be long and painful, and that only if the Bill was not given a second reading would they be spared a 'long hot summer of Parliamentary activity'.

The Shops Bill failed to receive a second reading by 296 votes to 282. No fewer than 72 Conservatives voted against the Bill.

THE SUNDAY TRADING BILL

Having promised to modernise Sunday shopping in the 1987 and 1992 manifestos, the Home Secretary, Kenneth Clark, announced that Parliament would be given a chance to vote on a series of options. MPs were to be given a free vote.

In July 1993, Home Office ministers produced a draft Bill for England and Wales, accompanied by a consultative paper 'Reforming the law on Sunday trading: a guide to the options for reform'. Options were the key to this attempt, as Clark had planned, though by then he had ceased to be Home Secretary, Michael Howard having replaced him. The draft Bill included three options which Clark had suggested:

1 *total deregulation*, removing all legal restrictions on the hours all shops should open, thereby effectively decriminalising any aspect of Sunday shopping;
2 *partial deregulation*, allowing all shops under 280 square metres (approximately 3,000 square feet) to open all day, and limiting larger ones to six hours;
3 *restricted trading*, providing a general ban on opening, but allowing specific exemptions for certain types of goods and shop.

The options debate, December 1993
The order of voting was important. Total deregulation was voted on at the beginning of the series and was defeated by 404 to 174. The most restrictive option was narrowly defeated by 18 votes (304 to 286). Partial deregulation was backed by 333 to 258.

LOBBYING MEMBERS OF PARLIAMENT

Rival pressure groups on either side of the argument fought a long and costly battle to win support for their point of view. Overall, it has been estimated that some £10 million was spent prior to the options vote.

Keep Sunday Special drew heavily on the 'expert' advice it could gather from bodies such as the Small Business Research Centre at the University of Cambridge concerning the potential effects of the repeal of Sunday trading laws on employment in the retail sector. It was alleged to have spent £3.5 million, some of it employed in the last few months by its own public relations staff and some by professional consultants.

The Retailers for Shops Act Reform was a coalition of large and small retailers set up in late 1992. It generally backed the Keep Sunday Special position but favoured allowing trade for the four Sundays before Christmas by those firms which wished to engage in it. Marks & Spencer was a prime mover in the organisation, but many well-known high-street stores were also represented: Aldi, Budgens, The Burton Group, CWS, Kwik Save, Littlewoods, Next and

Thorntons. The coalition made extensive use of Marks & Spencer's own staffing, but it also used the services of Shandwick and Market Access International (MAI). MAI specialised in campaigning for the retail sector, and its resources were directed towards briefing MPs.

In November 1993, Keep Sunday Special and Retailers for Shops Act Reform joined together in support of one option to satisfy the needs of consumers, retailers, employers and the community.

USDAW reacted to the changed circumstances of the period 1992–94, during which widespread illegal trading was unchecked by the local authorities and the government. Many thousands of its members volunteered to work for double-time rates. Moreover, a consultation exercise (July–October 1993) resulted in the basic proposition that a majority had no objection to companies having the right to open on Sunday, providing that working was voluntary and paid for at double-time.

On the other side, the main pressure group was the Shopping Hours Reform Council, a coalition of retailers established in 1988 to campaign for abolition of the Sunday trading laws. Several of the Shopping Hours Reform Council members were supermarkets and DIY stores, and a number of them were already trading illegally on Sundays, including B & Q. The Shopping Hours Reform Council was the only group to publish its accounts, which show that from the time of its launch it had spent £3.5 million. Part of this money was to hire the services of a public relations company, Burston Marsteller, which spearheaded the attempt to woo MPs and USDAW.

With the passage of the Bill in 1994, an answer had been found to a difficult problem on which ministers had been unable to find a consensus solution for several years.

Sources: Regan, P. (1988) 'The 1986 Shops Bill', in *Parliamentary Affairs*, Oxford University Press, Vol. 41, No. 2, pp 218–35; Bown, F. 'The defeat of the Shops Bill, 1986', in Rush, M. (ed) (1990) *Parliament and Pressure Politics*, Oxford: Clarendon Press; Watts, D. (1995) 'Sunday shopping: reform at last', in *Talking Politics*, The Politics Association, Vol. 8, No. 1, pp 45–52.

APPENDIX 3   THE EXPORT OF LIVE CALVES

The export of live animals from Britain had offended public sensibilities to become one of Britain's highest-profile animal-welfare campaigns in recent years. In 1995, thousands of people, predominantly from the South and South-east of England, took to the streets to register their revulsion at a trade which they perceived as barbaric, immoral and unnecessary. For many, it was to be their initial exposure to, and first personal experience of, protest activities. In November 1997, a petition advocating an end to live exports, spearheaded by Compassion in World Farming (CIWF), secured about 80,000 signatures. This was presented to Elliot Morley, minister responsible for animal welfare, by horse-racing commentator Sir Peter O'Sullevan. The campaign to ban live exports seems quite distinctive in relation to other animal-welfare campaigns because it had at times literally been brought home to members of the general public, as opposed to their having to initiate or manufacture an interest. This observation is particularly relevant to the residents of Brightlingsea (see below). The transportation of live farm animals through narrow residential streets in this town played a major part in bringing into public view what was previously hidden. Farm animals had become an urban spectacle.

BACKGROUND TO THE EXPORT OF LIVE ANIMALS

By raising public awareness, animal-welfare organisations play a major role in mobilising the public. They can activate public outrage and harness it to increase lobbying effectiveness. Channelling public feeling maximises the pressure that may be exerted on key participants in the trade. For example, in October 1994, two of the main ferry companies, P & O and Stena Link, announced that they would no longer ship live animals abroad. It would seem that considerable pressure had been exerted on the ferry companies through letters expressing opposition to the ferries' role in the export trade and threatening to boycott their passenger services. Exporters continued their business by chartering ships and aircraft, which meant that they had to negotiate access to minor seaports and airports. Ironically, this led to an intensification of the campaign, culminating in mass protests in places like Shoreham and Brightlingsea.

BRIGHTLINGSEA

In January 1995, the first convoy of lorries containing live animals arrived at the seaports of Shoreham and Brightlingsea. This development acted as a catalyst. Hundreds of people in the first town and thousands in the second took to the streets and blockaded the roads, and the lorries were initially turned back. They returned, however, the export trade continued, and the people resolutely continued to express their indignation.

The protests at Brightlingsea attracted unprecedented local, national and international media attention, much of which was generally sympathetic. The protests also occurred at a time when the campaign to ban live exports had been very much in the news the previous year. Thus, a climate had been created which meant that the media and the general public were both sensitive to the issue. Finally, the fact that the people involved in these protests challenged the media stereotype which had come to be associated with animal-welfare campaigns perhaps enabled 'ordinary' law-abiding people to identify with the protestors. This was exemplified by the plausible and articulate presentation of the spokesperson for the local protest group Brightlingsea Against Live Exports (BALE).

'NIMBY'ISM?

The residents of Brightlingsea did not have to initiate or manufacture an interest: the issue was brought to their doorsteps every weekday until October 1995 when the trade of live animals ceased going through their town. It was widely reported in the media that the protestors at Brightlingsea challenged the stereotype commonly associated with those active in the animal-rights movement. A survey conducted by McLeod in summer 1995 indicated that 82 per cent of the sample associated with BALE were female, 73 per cent were aged between 41 and 70, 38 per cent were retired, 71 per cent resided in the Brightlingsea area, and 80 per cent had never protested before. Since the export trade of live animals was thrust upon a town of approximately 8,000 residents without prior consultation, it could be argued that what arose was a NIMBY, that is Not In My Back Yard, response. However, it is interesting to note that when exports through Brightlingsea ceased, the local protest group continued to meet weekly, with 40 to 60 people attending on a regular basis. A further survey by McLeod in summer 1997 indicated that 76 per cent of them were female, 81 per cent were 50 years of age or over, and 55 per cent retired. BALE continued to update its telephone information lines on a daily basis and circulated its newsletter to supporters. In addition, coaches of demonstrators offered ongoing support to protestors at Dover, where export of live animals continued. They also travelled to other animal-welfare events in Britain and Europe. Some of the protestors regularly participated in watches at markets and lairages (temporary resting and feeding points for animals destined for market or export abroad), recording and if necessary reporting to officials – for example representatives of the veterinary profession, the Ministry of Agriculture or local authority Trading Standards services – any breaches in animal-welfare legislation. As a result, some of the participants became well informed about relevant legislation and were, in effect, voluntarily policing the system. The charge of NIMBYism fails to account adequately for the local residents who remained active well after the trade of live animals stopped going through their town.

THE LIVE FARM ANIMAL COMES INTO PUBLIC VIEW

Most people in urbanised Western societies have little direct contact with animals. Pet owners can act as mediators in this situation. They assume the responsibility of meeting their animals' physical needs, and this may help them understand the needs of livestock transported for export or sold at market. McLeod's 1997 survey showed that 71 per cent of respondents currently owned or looked after a pet, and that 90 per cent had at some time in their lives owned one.

The intensification of farming methods has been a significant factor in concealing farm animals from public view. When exporters had to find alternative seaports and airports following the ferry ban in 1994, their trade was much more evident. Dover is a 24-hour port accessed by dual carriageway, with the infrastructure to process convoys of lorries quickly.

At Brightlingsea, on the other hand, the only vehicular access to the wharf is a three-mile, narrow, winding road lined with residential houses and a few small businesses. The structure of the road became a resource for the protestors to generate media attention. In one incident, masses of sand, deposited in the road, had to be cleared before the lorries could get through. Moreover, Brightlingsea is more like a marina than a port. The transportation ship could only sail at certain times of the day, depending on the level of the tide. This had a bearing on who was able to protest. The afternoon made it difficult for people who were employed – predominantly men – to participate. Early morning or early evening allowed them to protest before going to work or on returning from work. Brightlingsea's infrastructure, combined with the mass protests, slowed down the procession of lorries carrying their cargo of live animals, making it difficult for witnesses to turn a blind eye.

Exposure to the trade increased public awareness of intensive farming methods, food production, European legislation and the economics which underpinned the trade.

THE VEAL-CRATE SYSTEM AND EUROPEAN LEGISLATION

The majority of male calves destined for the veal-crate system are an unwanted by-product of the dairy industry. In order to produce milk, cows have to produce calves. Female calves are reared to maintain milk production, but males have no value for the dairy farmer and are generally ill-suited for beef production. At about one week old, the latter begin their journey to the veal-crate system in continental Europe. The veal crate is a solid-sided wooden box with a slatted floor. Each calf is enclosed in a crate for the rest of its life, approximately 26 weeks. It is unable to turn round. No straw is provided because if consumed it could alter the colour of the veal from the preferred white to a pale pink. The calf is fed a reconstituted liquid diet, with reduced iron content, also to ensure that the flesh remains pale.

In January 1995, CIWF launched an investigative video made by a freelance filmmaker and a former BBC environment correspondent. They had followed a consignment of calves from Coventry Airport to Rennes Airport, then shadowed trucks to a veal-crate system somewhere in France. Video footage, depicting the calves 'struggling against their chains, frightened and desperate', was shown on national television and attracted widespread newspaper coverage. Consequently, the people involved in the protests at Brightlingsea had certainly become more informed about the conditions and farming practices which would meet the calves at their destination.

The high-profile public demonstrations at the local grass-roots level provided a tremendous opportunity for animal-welfare organisations such as CIWF to lobby for legislative changes at a European level.

It is important to note that the campaign to ban live exports has not been promoted as a 'veggie issue'. According to McLeod's 1997 survey, of those who continued to attend BALE's weekly meeting, 64 per cent continued to eat meat, fish or chicken. This enabled the campaigners to mobilise a wider base of public support, as in a poster: 'You Don't Have To Stop Eating Meat To Care – Ban Live Exports.' It seems that those who were more ideologically orientated, that is who adopted a more animal-rights perspective and were more likely to be vegetarian or vegan, tended to assume a more proactive role in the campaign. However, it could also be argued that as the issue was transported to the residents of Brightlingsea, it engaged people who would campaign because of an interest in animal-related issues since they were unable to turn a blind eye.

CONCLUSION

The protests generated by the campaign to ban live exports appear to illustrate that the activity of protesting has become increasingly acceptable socially as a mechanism which enables 'ordinary' members of the public to communicate and register their concern to governmental bodies.

Source: McLeod, R. (1998) 'Calf exports at Brightlingsea', in *Parliamentary Affairs*, Oxford University Press, Vol. 51, No. 3, pp. 345–57.

APPENDIX 4   THE ANTI-ORGANOPHOSPHOROUS [OP] CAMPAIGN

The regulation of pesticides has been politically controversial and provided fertile ground for pressure-group activity throughout the industrialised world. Pesticides and veterinary medicines include a wide variety of biologically active and dangerous substances which are designed to control diseases in crops and animals. The modern use of organophosphorous (OP) compounds in agriculture developed from the work of scientists in Germany in the 1930s and 1940s, work which more disturbingly contributed to the development of chemical weapons and nerve gases. Concern was already evident 50 years ago about the impact on wildlife, but there has been increasing worry about the potential adverse effects on humans of low-level, long-term exposure. There has also been much speculation about a connection to 'Gulf War Syndrome', and to the suicide in 1997 of Gordon McMaster, the Labour MP, who himself linked his tiredness, depression and severe mood swings to over-exposure to OP pesticides during his work as a gardener.

In its concern with dangerous chemical products such as OPs, the role of the State is essentially regulatory. A wide range of interests are involved in a complex administrative system – industrial manufacturers, workers, farmers, environmentalists and domestic users. The Ministry of Agriculture is the lead department for the approval and supply of agricultural pesticides and veterinary medicines, working through its executive agencies. On the other hand, the Health and Safety Executive, an agency of the Department of Education and Employment, oversees the reporting of incidents and the use of hazardous substances in the workplace; responsibility for checking compliance with regulations rests primarily with its agricultural inspectors.

There are two parallel administrative structures for pesticides and veterinary medicines. OP compounds are used in a wide range of agricultural products, but sheep dips are regulated as veterinary medicines rather than pesticides because the matter is classed as one of animal health. This has some important implications: while the pesticides-approval process is relatively open, that for veterinary medicines is subject to the strict confidentiality provisions of the Medicines Act. Overall policy on OP sheep-dips lies with the Ministry of Agriculture in conjunction with the Health departments, acting on the advice of an independent Veterinary Products Committee of scientific experts such as vets, pharmacists and toxicologists. The main administrative institution is the Veterinary Medicines Directorate, now an executive agency. This has a general duty to ensure the safety, quality and efficacy of veterinary medicines in Britain safeguarding the health and safety of farmers, workers, consumers and the environment generally as well as that of animals.

OPs AND PUBLIC PROTEST

Essentially, the protest campaign has been directed at the use of a small number of sheep-dip products containing OP chemicals. The campaign has been persistent, regionalised and relatively low key, but has flared into general public consciousness on several occasions. Although the number of individuals who have reported health problems as a result of OP exposure is measured in hundreds rather than thousands, the issue arouses much wider concern amongst workers manufacturing the products, users such as farmers and gardeners, doctors and other health specialists, consumers worried about residues in meat, and those concerned more generally with the adverse environmental effects of chemical use.

At the core of the protest have been those lobby and self-help groups organised to assist individuals who are convinced that their health has been directly affected by OPs. Most notable in this respect have been the Organophosphates Information Network, the National Action Group and Pesticides Exposure Group of Sufferers. The last, established in 1988 and based in Cambridge, has provided counselling for sufferers and publicised the issue. The National Action Group was set up in 1991 to press for recognition of the problem by a Devon farmer forced to quit the industry because of health problems associated with OP use. Also reflecting the geographic location of many of the reported cases, the Cornwall-based Organophosphates Information Network has campaigned strongly, arranging meetings, counselling and acting as a focal point for sheep farmers who have suffered from chronic ill-health through OPs, and has been an important information resource. It has also acted as a political protest group, coordinating the input of a growing number of sympathetic scientists, lawyers, doctors and journalists. There have also been links with the various groups representing Gulf War veterans. The approach, therefore, has combined voluntary action and protest with more conventional political tactics. Small demonstrations have occasionally been mounted outside places to be visited by ministers, but much emphasis has been put on the collection of reliable case data and scientific evidence which can be presented to the relevant authorities.

The OP issue was initially contained within established political parameters, as for example with the submission by Mark Purdey, the Somerset farmer who was one of the first to draw attention to the issue, to the Agriculture Committee's 1987 investigation into the effects of pesticides on human health. However, the issue has impinged more directly on wider public consciousness, demonstrated by significant media exposure in popular press, radio and television. Much press coverage of the effects of OPs followed the death of Gordon McMaster MP and also surrounded the debate about Gulf War Syndrome.

More conventional political channels have also been used. The issue has been aired frequently in Parliament, both in the investigations of the Agriculture

Committee and in debates and questions. Sympathetic MPs such as Tom King and Jean Corston have voiced a concern which transcends party boundaries and which reflects its relevance to region and constituency. Anti-OP campaigners were also lucky in that the Countess of Mar, a sheep farmer who herself had suffered from OP exposure, was able to exploit her membership of the House of Lords to highlight the issue. While some have regarded judicial action as inappropriate because of the difficulty of identifying liability, negligence and causation, claims on behalf of members for compensation against employers have been increasing. It is also likely that many cases have been settled out of court. For example, in February 1998, a shepherd represented by Unison obtained an £80,500 out-of-court settlement from Lancashire County Council.

THE VESTED INTERESTS

For many critics of OP use, the villains of the peace are those stuck on the treadmill of industrial agriculture: the Ministry of Agriculture, the chemical industries and the NFU. Indeed, it is partly the difficulty of challenging such entrenched interests successfully which has led many of the campaigners against OP use to find alternative channels of expression. As the organisation representing many of those affected or at risk, it might be expected that the NFU would be at the forefront of the anti-OP campaign. In fact, it has experienced acute internal difficulties as grass-roots pressure and mounting other evidence have forced it to take the OP issue seriously. It sponsored a joint seminar with the British Medical Association (BMA) in June 1995, at which its leadership was subjected to sustained criticism from the floor, and there was a groundswell of opinion in favour of a ban amongst those who attended. Much of the protest came from farmers in south-western counties, where the NFU regional director was well known for his anti-OP views. However, the problem for the NFU leadership was that most sheep farmers had suffered no ill-effects.

So, the leadership of the NFU has maintained support for a policy of industrial agriculture based on the continued use of chemicals. Its leadership has declared confidence in the existing regulatory system. While the concerns about OP sheep-dips have been taken seriously, the NFU has pointed out that the relevant compounds are licensed and very useful to farmers. If serious adverse effects have been proved to result from their proper use, then they would be banned through the regulatory process, just as other dangerous substances have been withdrawn in the past. It has therefore tried to reassure members, while providing regular advice on sheep dips to make farmers more aware of the symptoms of exposure, and encouraging the use of protective clothing. It has also promoted research into the effects of OP exposure as well as into safer alternatives.

If the organisation representing most sheep farmers has been somewhat ambivalent on the OP issue, no such uncertainties have beset those who manufacture the products. For pesticides and veterinary medicines, there are influential organisations representing manufacturing companies, the British Agrochemicals Association for the former and the National Office of Animal Health for the latter. They have maintained that what is important is accurate information, a choice of products and the minimisation of risk rather than a total ban on OP sheep-dips. Clearly, any successful campaign against OPs would threaten the profits of the manufacturing companies concerned, and they have therefore lobbied strenuously against stricter controls, arguing that the costs of more regulation would threaten the availability of a wide range of affordable animal medicines.

For some people, there has been an unhealthily close relationship between the Ministry of Agriculture and the manufacturing companies, with the NFU making up the unholy trinity. Fears of regulatory capture have been heightened by the fact that much of the funding of the approvals and licensing work of the Veterinary Medicines Directorate has come from the pharmaceutical industry. For example, there has been unease about the location, in the same agency, of responsibility for the approval of veterinary medicines and the investigation of adverse health effects. Some have argued that this has made the ministry reluctant to promote a reduction in chemical usage. Trade unions have tended to argue that responsibility for safety aspects of regulation should be given to the Health and Safety Executive to avoid potential conflicts of interest, together with more resources for enforcement.

PUBLIC PROTEST AND PROFESSIONAL OPINION

Established political forums have also been challenged by the anti-OP campaign in another important way. It has been a matter not simply of using unconventional techniques but also of calling into question the very procedures themselves through which official decisions are taken. Regulation of dangerous chemical products, such as those contained in pesticides and animal medicines, has always been fundamentally technocratic. Scientific research and expertise are of crucial importance in many areas of government policy. Dependence upon experts to interpret ambiguous, if not contradictory evidence influences both the nature of the policy process and the manner in which problems are understood. As a result, the debate on OPs has reflected a fundamental dispute about the role of government in complex technical areas, about the role of scientific research and advice, and about the relative value of scientific knowledge and lay expertise. Government policy on OPs has relied heavily on the experts: the advice of committees such as the Veterinary Products Committee has been invariably accepted.

Critics of the use of OPs have questioned first the 'burden of proof' argument. What is needed is a 'precautionary approach' which recognises the limits of scientific knowledge. Users, workers, consumers and the environment must therefore be given the benefit of the doubt, and dangerous products should only be approved when all reasonable concerns about their safety have been removed.

The second strand of the argument about scientific expertise, sometimes called the democratic critique, holds that 'the primary problem is the failure of the regulatory agencies to incorporate a full enough range of values into their decision making' (Jasanoff). This is allied to criticism of the cloak of secrecy which surrounds the British policy process. The democratic response is for more lay representation on scientific advisory committees and for a more open and accessible decision-making process.

Although the voice of environmental and public health groups and of consumer interests has become increasingly heard in Britain, the policy community on relatively invisible issues such as veterinary medicines remains closed and specialist. It is vital for opponents of OPs to open out and democratise the debate, not least because the well-resourced manufacturing interests are able to control the research agenda within the narrow confines of established technocratic structures. This situation has been exacerbated by the decrease in state funding which means that research expenditure is increasingly met by the chemical industry itself.

For many critics, therefore, it is the conventional technocratic approach itself which has contributed to the emergence of serious problems such as the adverse health effects of exposure to OP products. Indeed, in a 1987 report, the House of Commons Agriculture Committee drew unfavourable comparisons between the British regulatory system and those in the USA and Canada, characterised by greater openness and the incorporation of a wider range of interests. As early as 1981, the Health and Safety Commission drew attention to the need to involve representatives of users, workers and the community generally in the risk-evaluation process, alongside the scientific experts. The TGWU has campaigned for formal and effective representation for those with experience of problems in the field, including worker and consumer representatives, environmentalists and developmental bodies. Even the National Office of Animal Health has argued for outside observer seats on expert committees in order to allay suspicions about regulatory capture and give assurance about the operation of the system.

Source: Greer, A. (1998) 'Pesticides, sheep dips and science', in *Parliamentary Affairs*, Oxford University Press, Vol. 51, No. 3, pp. 411–23.

APPENDIX 5   THE SNOWDROP CAMPAIGN

On the morning of 13 March 1996, Thomas Hamilton, a licensed gun holder, entered the local primary school in Dunblane, shooting a number of rounds at a class of children in the gymnasium. As a result, 16 young pupils and their teacher were killed, with only 13 of the class surviving.

Until March 1996, the worst single act of mass murder in Britain had been that of the 'Hungerford Massacre' where Michael Ryan killed 16 people in 1987, and although outrage over this particular tragic incident was great, the government response, in terms of legislation, was not. While a review of gun control and licensing was conducted then, the changes advocated and implemented were considered by some not to be sufficiently far-reaching, and the feeling was that the government had given way to the pro-gun lobby.

The immediate aftermath of the Dunblane massacre saw the birth of the Snowdrop Appeal, created by a number of concerned families in central Scotland, but not by the parents of the victims. Anne Pearston and a friend of one of the families decided to do something to prevent the recurrence of such an event, and in discussion with a member of her yoga class, the idea of a petition came into being. The name 'Snowdrop' was adopted because it was the only flower in bloom at the time of the shootings. So Pearston and a few others launched the petition which called for the banning of the private ownership of handguns. Martin O'Neil, Pearston's Labour MP, provided advice on how to set up a parliamentary petition, but a key feature of the appeal in its early stages was its apolitical nature. None of the group had been political in the past, and their knowledge of the British political system and political lobbying was minimal. This was a genuine local community group that grew beyond the intentions of its founders.

The first stage began simply with the group setting up a pasting table outside a shopping centre in Stirling, with copies of the petition for shoppers to sign. Originally, the Appeal was to be anonymous and unrelated to the families of the victims. Out of respect for the families of the victims, copies of the petition were not sent to the town, though a number of Dunblane families did sign it. The petition was, however, taken to a string of other Scottish towns, including Edinburgh. One of the bereaved parents, Dr Mick North, appeared at the launch of the Appeal. He also accompanied the campaign to lobby MPs at the Scottish Grand Committee in Inverness. Subsequent to the launch and its support by a number of the families of the victims, the Snowdrop Appeal, in the eyes of the public and the media, became organically linked with the tragedy of Dunblane.

The media adoption of the Appeal, and the subsequent campaign by *The Sunday Mail*, *Sun* and *Sunday Times* amongst other newspapers, ensured that Snowdrop grew from its original intentions. From its inception, it sought merely to demonstrate public support for the control of guns by a petition to the government. During 1996, its degree of politicisation grew as the pro-gun lobby mustered arguments against the tightening of gun laws and MPs came forward to state their own positions on the issue, with both sides of the argument finding support. The Conservative government set up the Cullen Inquiry into the tragedy, and its remit included the current state of legislation relating to the control and licensing of firearms. Politicians began to comment on the situation by indicating how far their personal support would extend in relation to a total ban on guns. The issue, much discussed in the media, moved up the political agenda, and with it climbed support for the increasingly politicised Snowdrop campaign.

THE CAMPAIGN

Originally, the Snowdrop Appeal and the parents of Dunblane called for the tightening of gun control and the safe storage of recreational firearms at gun clubs, but the debate soon became polarised, with demands for a total ban on handguns. The petition called for changes in the law so that

> *all firearms held for recreational purposes for use in authorised sporting clubs be held securely at such clubs with the firing mechanisms removed; the private ownership of handguns be made illegal; certification of all firearms be subject to stricter control.*

It neatly summarised the arguments against changing the gun laws, and put forward its response to them. A copy was sent out to every school in mainland Britain by the Scottish Schools Boards for parents to make copies of it. It was supported by the Scottish National Party and the National Union of Teachers.

The group itself had no formal organisation, but Anne Pearston became its effective head because of her media profile. It was largely run by volunteers with little free time because of their family commitments, but that did not appear to hinder activities. One of its first actions was a newspaper advertisement with a tear-off slip that could be sent to the then Prime Minister, John Major, calling for a total ban.

The events that followed Dunblane ensured that the pressure would increase on Parliament to alter the law relating to gun control. On 19 March, two youths were arrested for the theft of four firearms from a private house in Buckinghamshire. A number of schools in the area were alerted despite a statement by Thames Valley Police noting that while charges against the youths were not likely, it was not seeking any other people in connection with the theft. The Thames Valley Assistant Chief Constable stated that unarmed plain-clothes officers had attended three local schools in order to reassure teachers, parents and children after news broke of the search for the guns and the youths. While there was no evidence or intelligence to suggest that schools might have been a target, they decided certain schools would be offered whatever protection they deemed necessary.

The reporting of this event and the reaction to it ensured that individual MPs would not remain silent as had been suggested shortly after Dunblane (as a mark of respect for the families of the victims). On 20 March, David Mellor, a former Home Office minister, led demands for radical changes to the existing legislation, commenting that events in Buckinghamshire had once again highlighted the total inadequacy of the existing controls and the need for immediate legislative action.

Both Conservative and Labour backbenchers demanded early action on the ownership of handguns such as those used by Thomas Hamilton in Dunblane, and on the storing of firearms in private homes. These were similar reactions to those after the Hungerford massacre, when reviews of firearm controls banned the keeping of weapons such as those used by Michael Ryan, but little more. After Dunblane, the calls for change grew in strength partly as a result of the perceived failure to act adequately then. George Foulkes, Labour MP for Carrick, Cummnock and Doone Valley, said there was a 'growing tide in favour of outlawing handguns' and 'also growing support for handguns, but not shotguns, to be held at gun clubs rather than in private homes'. The debate had quickly shifted from whether there should be changes in the law to what form such changes should take. Party lines began to emerge in what had previously been a non-partisan issue, with the Labour Party pressing for a parliamentary debate, and this was endorsed by George Robertson, Shadow Secretary of State for Scotland and a resident of Dunblane. Twenty-eight people, including relatives of the victims, went to London to deliver the petition in July. They were received by the Home Secretary and by the Prime Minister, Tony Blair.

While debate over the extent of reform raged in anticipation of the Cullen Report, the government offered an interim gesture to demonstrate its commitment to firearms control. In an attempt to reduce the number of unauthorised guns, an amnesty was offered from 3 to 30 June. Gun amnesties were not new, and this merely suggested a hurried response to public opinion. It did nothing to stem the tide of popular opinion.

Public perception was likely to attribute much of the success in gun control to the Snowdrop Appeal, its public statements, the work of the Dunblane parents, and, in particular, Ann Pearston, who spearheaded an attempt to force the government's hand by declaring her intention to stand against it in a general election should it fail to implement radical changes in gun control. Conversely, media reporting of the emotive responses of MPs suggests that the issue was taken to heart by Parliament and that changes would have been precipitated in any case. Legislative reform had been proposed unsuccessfully the previous year by Terry Lewis (Labour) who had called for a ban on keeping guns on domestic premises. Arguably, Dunblane acted as the catalyst on an issue about which Parliament was already aware. This suggests that the effect of the Snowdrop Appeal on parliamentary debate and legislation was useful but not as decisive as may have appeared.

The Cullen Report was published in September 1996. It was wide-ranging in its scope, covering gun clubs, gun licences, safety in schools, etc, but narrow in its recommendations. By that time, however, it had already been overtaken by other events. Together with the Labour Party's decision to support a total ban, this made the Report, which in any case fell short of the campaign's demands, almost irrelevant.

THE LEGISLATION

The imminence of a general election, with its likelihood of coming close to the first anniversary of the tragedy, not only put the controversial issue of gun control firmly on the political agenda but also placed pressure on the government to have legislation in place before the election, and preferably before the anniversary.

In the days following the massacre, party leaders had agreed not to exploit the issue politically, nor to speculate on possible political outcomes. They agreed to await the findings of the Cullen Inquiry. However, consensus broke down some two months before the publication of the Cullen Report, with a series of leaks from the House of Commons Select Committee on Home Affairs report of August 1996, *Possession of Handguns*. The Conservative-dominated Committee concluded that a ban was not necessary, but with the Labour minority supporting a ban. This created a great deal of controversy for the government. The tabloid press strongly supported a ban, characterised by *The Sun's* attack which printed the telephone numbers of Conservative members of the Committee and suggested that readers might like to ring them to complain about their conclusions. BBC television broadcast a 50-minute *Panorama* programme which interviewed the parents of victims who criticised the Select Committee. The government could have been left in no doubt as to the depth of feeling over the issue.

The Snowdrop campaign announced that it would put up candidates in the 10 Conservative-held Scottish seats in the General Election unless the government obtained a total ban on handguns in Parliament before then. It then dropped the idea of candidates, pledging its support to the Labour Party instead.

The government declared itself for the banning of all handguns except those used specifically for sport in secure gun clubs. This seemed to satisfy no-one. The gun lobby felt that its members were being made to pay for the crime of one man, while the anti-gun lobby was not satisfied with a partial ban because legally held weapons could still be misused.

The Firearms (Amendment) Act was given Royal Assent on 27 February, and became law on 3 March, 1997. It prohibited all handguns other than small-calibre pistols, muzzle-loading guns and signalling apparatus. Exemptions were made for guns used in slaughterhouses, those used for the humane killing of animals, starting guns in sports events, and guns acquired before 1946 as a trophy of war. Firearms certificates could be granted for the ownership of small-calibre (.22 or less) pistols as long as they were housed and used in licensed, secure gun clubs. Certificate holders were required to be members of a licensed club. Special permits could be granted by the chief office of police for the restricted use of small-calibre pistols outside gun clubs, primarily for competitive target shooting. The legislation provided for compensation to gun owners surrendering their prohibited firearms and ammunition. It set out new requirements for the granting, renewal and revocation of firearm certificates, and new requirements for applications for such certificates, with two referees providing a much wider range of information than previously. Greater powers were given to the courts and police concerning the entry and search of premises.

THE MEDIA

The traditionally powerful and well-resourced influence of the gun lobby, whose influence was seen after the Hungerford massacre, meant that the anti-gun campaigners stood little chance of achieving their objectives without over-whelming popular support. The Snowdrop campaign started out as a simple petition, without funding or sophisticated organisation, and with its organisers tending to remain anonymous. If this had remained the case, it might have sank quietly once its petition had been submitted to the Prime Minister. However, not only did the media support make the Snowdrop petition difficult for the government to ignore, it also forced the gun lobby to seek legitimacy in the public arena.

THE 1997 ELECTION AND BEYOND

The more openly political approach adopted during the 1997 election campaign was an attempt to achieve a change in government and, with it, a handgun ban.

A Labour government was elected on 1 May 1997. The commitment to banning handguns was in the Queen's Speech at the opening of the new Parliament. On 27 May, a bill was given its first reading in Parliament to ban all handguns, including those .22 calibre and smaller that had been exempted under the previous legislation, as well as to revoke the possibility of owners holding their guns on club premises. The new law gained Royal Assent on 27 November 1997, and came into force on 26 January 1998.

Source: Thomson, S., Stancich, L. and Dickson, L. (1998) 'Gun control and Snowdrop', in *Parliamentary Affairs*, Oxford University Press, Vol. 51, No. 3, pp. 329–44.

APPENDIX 6   DRURIDGE BAY CAMPAIGNS

Druridge Bay is a six-mile-long stretch of Northumbrian coastline, 20 miles north of Newcastle. For most of the year, it is a windswept wilderness. When the weather is less inclement, it attracts people from all over the region because of its isolation and natural beauty. The Bay contains four nature reserves, includes a Site of Special Scientific Interest, and is just to the south of the designated Area of Natural Beauty running down the coast from Berwick to Amble. The vicinity of the Bay is not untouched by industrialisation, mostly opencast coal mining, though by now most of the old mineworkings have been restored to farmland or turned into nature reserves.

OPPOSING NUCLEAR POWER

The news, three days before Christmas 1978, that Druridge Bay was being considered by the Central Electricity Generating Board as a possible site for a Pressurised Water Rector (PWR) nuclear-power station led to the formation of a pressure group, the Druridge Bay Association, in March 1979. The participants were mostly people living in the immediate vicinity of the proposed development, with the central protagonists drawn from the 'educated middle class', including a teacher, a manager, an engineer, a scientist and a librarian. A few were also members of environmental and civic groups, but the motivation for collective action was based largely on the perceived threat to the individuals and their immediate locality (that is on a NIMBY response) rather than on any ideological commitment to green issues or opposition to nuclear power in principle.

The Association had some success in mobilising public protest despite having limited resources. It attracted support from one of the local district councils, Castle Morpeth, but not from the Northumberland County Council, which adopted a 'wait and see' approach at this stage. The Association realised that its campaign would be strengthened enormously by County Council support, and its primary aim was to secure this. It published a pamphlet setting out the case against nuclear power, and circulated this locally. A petition was also launched opposing the development, which eventually attracted around 30,000 signatures, 1 in 10 of the adult population of Northumberland. The Association organised large public gatherings, including a rally of 3,000 people at the Bay in July 1979. It also participated in public consultation meetings on the issue, attracting local media attention in the process. Finally, it sought to win support from MPs, trade unions, environmental and anti-nuclear pressure groups, conservation groups and civic societies.

In 1980, this pressure paid off as Northumberland County Council came out against the proposed development, but this did not prevent the Central

Electricity Generating Board embarking on a series of drilling tests at the site, and in December that year the site was declared viable for a PWR nuclear-power station. Meanwhile, Britain's first proposed PWR, at Sizewell in Suffolk, was to be the subject of a public inquiry, and this, coupled with a further public inquiry regarding the planned PWR at Hinkley in Somerset, presented additional opportunities for opponents of the Druridge scheme to participate in the nuclear-power debate. For example, two of the local authorities involved, Wansbeck District Council and Northumberland County Council, made representations at the Sizewell public inquiry.

Although there was a great deal of local opposition to the development, a number of competing perspectives arose. Despite their common interests, civic groups, anti-nuclear protestors, conservation and environmental groups, local authorities and trade unions were unable or unwilling to work together on the issue. Tentative moves to overcome these differences came to nothing, and the Association began to run out of steam. Between 1981 and 1983, the campaign became almost moribund, even though the nuclear-power 'threat' remained ever-present. In 1982, news that Druridge Bay was on a shortlist of six sites focused minds on the need to reinvigorate the campaign and improve coordination between local groups. A key factor was the creation of a local FoE group in 1983, which led to a more effective link between local green activists and local councils. Another was the networking of anti-nuclear activists on Tyneside within local trade unions, which brought these organisations firmly behind the campaign. Eventually, in 1984, the strands of opposition were brought together in a new pressure group, the Druridge Bay Campaign, a federation of 38 organisations with an individual membership of 500 people. It was funded by contributions from the constituent groups, which included trade unions and local authorities, and later, individual subscriptions as well, and was led by a committee representing the major players.

The creation of the Druridge Bay Campaign, which attracted considerable publicity from local press and television, began to mobilise opinion more effectively. After the Central Electricity Generating Board bought out properties near the proposed development in 1984, the Campaign moved up another gear. Local opposition was demonstrated in public rallies throughout 1985, as well as at special events at the Bay.

One of the key turning points occurred in 1986 when the Chernobyl disaster produced widespread fear about the safety of nuclear power, particularly in areas earmarked for nuclear sites. Campaign members independently monitored the Chernobyl effect and were deluged with requests from the public and the media throughout the North-east who were desperate for data on possible contamination. During 1986, the organisation was strengthened with the recruitment of a part-time publicity officer and a part-time education officer, while sufficient income was raised, mainly from local authorities, to provide separate office facilities. These new arrangements were essential for the next phase of the Campaign. With the approval of Sizewell B in 1987, the Druridge Bay Campaign began to focus greater attention on national lobbying. By now, almost all the local authorities in the region had declared their support for the Campaign, and the local media and public opinion were also strongly behind it. The Campaign also won explicit support from almost all MPs in the region, with Alan Beith (Liberal Democrat, Berwick) and Jack Thompson (Labour, Wansbeck) being particularly active on its behalf.

Opportunities to lobby at a national level were increased by the Thatcher government's decision to privatise the electricity industry. The passage of this legislation enabled all the local and national groups opposed to nuclear power to attract a wider audience. It also gave them an opportunity to persuade MPs to introduce amendments to the legislation in an effort to undermine the expansion of nuclear power. Given the government's large parliamentary majority, these amendments were unlikely to succeed, but they at least ensured that the case for nuclear power would be critically debated in public. In November 1988, FoE organised a national lobby of Parliament, bringing together the various local protest groups, which attracted considerable publicity. Throughout the passage of the bill, local MPs and peers were lobbied in an effort to put pressure on the government. One notable victory was a House of Lords amendment requiring the privatised electricity companies to promote energy efficiency. Although diluted by the House of Commons, it attracted further publicity for those who argued that an expansion of nuclear power was unnecessary given the potential for energy conservation.

The situation then changed drastically, the nuclear-power stations being suddenly withdrawn from the electricity privatisation programme after the government's own financial advisers found that nuclear-waste disposal and decommissioning costs were higher than previously estimated. Moreover, the government placed a moratorium on the building of new nuclear-power stations pending a review of the industry.

This review, completed in 1994, confirmed that no more nuclear-power stations would be built with public-sector support. Subsequently, in 1996, the nuclear-power industry was part-privatised, with the older Magnox reactors remaining in the public sector. In the meantime, the Druridge Bay Campaign maintained pressure on the government.

Campaigners believed that it was vital that the land still owned by the nuclear industry did not end up in the hands of the privatised company British Energy. Magnox Electric, the public-sector body responsible for the older rump of the industry, was given the land. Following persistent lobbying from the Druridge Bay Campaign, it announced in November 1996 that it was selling the site for agricultural or residential use.

SAND EXTRACTION

Northern Aggregates, a subsidiary of Ready Mixed Concrete, was engaged in sand extraction at the Bay. This became an important issue for the Campaign and its affiliated organisations in 1990. They believed that excessive quantities of sand were being taken from the site, causing disruption to those wishing to use the Bay as an amenity, to wildlife and to people living on the main access routes. Problems associated with coastal erosion were also attributed to the cumulative effects of extraction.

As with the anti-nuclear power campaign, the local authorities were useful allies, and they continued to provide financial resources. A public campaign was launched, including a petition which eventually attracted some 20,000 signatures, and events aimed at attracting publicity, for example a beach party.

The Campaign adopted King Canute as a symbolic character, with members dressing up to attract publicity in various locations, for example outside the Department of the Environment and the offices of Ready Mixed Concrete. This new approach refreshed the media's presentation of the Campaign, thereby maintaining interest locally.

Meanwhile on the parliamentary front, local MPs began to lobby the Department of the Environment on the issue. Parliamentary Questions were asked, and an adjournment debate was raised. Following this, with encouragement from the government, Ready Mixed Concrete opened a dialogue with the Campaign and the local authorities. In 1993, it stated that it would agree to a phased withdrawal from the Bay, but only if alternative sites could be found in the region.

The failure to find alternative sites meant that extraction at Druridge Bay continued. Then, in 1996, Ready Mixed Concrete announced the cessation of its activities at the Bay, abandoning this relatively small but profitable extraction site 56 years earlier than legally obliged to do so.

This decision was announced a week after the decision by Magnox Electric to sell the site earmarked for the nuclear-power station.

Source: Baggott, R. (1998) 'Nuclear power at Druridge Bay', in *Parliamentary Affairs*, Oxford University Press, Vol. 51, No. 3, pp384–96.

APPENDIX 7   BRENT SPAR

Since the mid-1960s, the North Sea has been the site of significant industrial activity. Over the 30 years after oil extraction began, approximately 400 production and storage platforms had been put in place. However, the nature of oil as a depleting resource and commercial pressures to reduce costs had led to the situation where the decommissioning of the first of those platforms was now in hand.

The Brent Spar storage and loading buoy was to have been the first of these 400 to be disposed of, by Shell. Of this number, only 50 platforms could be considered for off-shore abandonment: legal guidelines required the remaining platforms and installations to be dismantled due to either their smaller size or their shallow moorings. Herein lies one major reason why Greenpeace took direct action against the mode of disposal, which was to be dumping in the North Atlantic, 150 miles off Scotland. As the first of the 400, Brent Spar took on an enormous symbolic significance.

The second major reason why Greenpeace became involved again concerns the mode of disposal. There has been significant debate within the scientific community over the scale and nature of the impact on the marine environment were Brent Spar to be disposed of in the deep waters of the Atlantic. In addition to this, for many in the environmental movement, dumping would send the wrong signals to both industry and the population at large at a time when they were being entreated to stop viewing the environment as a convenient and free repository for the externalities of industrial society. A final reason that has been suggested for Greenpeace's intervention in the disposal of Brent Spar concerns its image over recent years. Some of the observers of the environmental movement (and also some of its members) had argued that Greenpeace had moved away from its campaigning style and become too 'professionalised', concerned with its own maintenance rather than with taking direct action to protect the environment. From this perspective, Brent Spar provided Greenpeace with an opportunity both to re-establish its credentials as a direct-action organisation and to reverse what had been a declining membership in Britain.

THE TIMETABLE OF EVENTS

The roots of the Brent Spar episode lie in September 1991 when the structure was decommissioned, and the major events are shown chronologically in Table 17. Between 1991 and February 1995, the process was essentially a private one involving Shell UK, the government and those selected for consultation. With the government's announcement of its intention to approve deep-water disposal, the process moved into the public arena. Greenpeace argued that the oil company's estimates of the toxic materials remaining on the installation were inaccurate.

Accordingly, the pressure group set about mounting a very high-profile campaign on the Brent Spar, inviting reporters from both the print and electronic media to accompany the Greenpeace activists when they initially occupied the platform in April 1995, also providing editing and platform-to-shore communications facilities for the media.

Table 17: *Chronology of the Brent Spar*	
DATE	MAJOR EVENTS
1991 Sept	Brent Spar decommissioned
Oct	Abandonment studies commence
1992	Shell begins discussion with regulatory authorities over disposal options
1993	Scientific studies ongoing
1994 Feb	Aberdeen University study endorses deep-water disposal. Shell consults with conservation bodies and fishing interests
Oct	Final draft of 'Best Practicable Environmental Option' and 'Impact Hypothesis' submitted to the Dept of Trade and Industry
1995 Feb	Government announces intention to approve deep-water disposal and notifies relevant European governments
30 Apr	Greenpeace occupies Brent Spar
5 May	Government issues the disposal licence
9 May	German Government lodges a protest with the British Government over the plan to dump at sea
23 May	Greenpeace activists removed from Brent Spar and picketing of Shell petrol station forecourts begins
8–9 June	Esbjerg meeting of North Sea Ministerial Conference
10 June	Shell UK begin to tow Brent Spar to disposal site
15–17 June	Chancellor Kohl of Germany protests to John Major at the G7 summit over disposal plans
15–20 June	Vociferous protests at Shell's German service stations
20 June	John Major defends Shell and, during Prime Minister's Question Time, supports the dumping of Brent Spar in the Atlantic
	Shell decides to abort the operation and Brent Spar begins to make the return journey
7 July	Permission granted by Norwegian Government to moor the Brent Spar in fjord while reappraisal carried out

SOURCE: SHELL, BRENT SPAR, AND GENERAL MEDIA SOURCES.

Following the eviction of Greenpeace's activists on 23 May, and the beginning of the installation's journey to the dumping site, the pressure group shadowed the progress of the 14,500-tonne, 463 ft former oil-storage and loading buoy by both ship and helicopter. The resulting pictures were meat and drink to the news media.

The impact of these pictures on public opinion was considerable, and Shell came under pressure to change its decision, the most public expression of this pressure coming through the picketing of its service stations in much of Northern Europe. Feelings in Germany, where green issues had been salient since the early 1980s, ran high. There were physical attacks on 50 service stations in Germany, of which two were firebombed and one subjected to gunfire. This public pressure was matched on 8 and 9 June at the fourth North Sea Ministerial Conference held in Esbjerg by calls from all of Britain's European partners except Norway to dispose of decommissioned installations on land, and by protests from Chancellor Kohl of Germany to British Prime Minister Major at the G7 summit a week later. Ultimately, on 20 June 1995, Shell UK bowed to the intense pressure to which it had been subjected and announced that it would no longer seek to dispose of the Spar at sea but would re-evaluate its options. Angered by the oil company's about-face and the subsequent embarrassment caused to it, the British government indicated that there was no guarantee that a licence to dispose of Brent Spar on land would be forthcoming. This embarrassment was compounded by the fact that on 20 June, Major had made a statement supporting Shell's disposal option and condemning those who sought to have it disposed of on land as irresponsible, only to find a few hours later that the oil company had decided to reconsider its line of action. As an interim measure, the Norwegian government offered to allow Shell to moor the platform in a deep-water fjord until its fate could be decided.

Greenpeace apologised to Shell for a mistake that had been made by its activists when they had sampled the oil-storage tanks on the Brent Spar. Instead of sampling the tanks, the measuring instrument had become stuck in the pipe leading to the tanks, leading to an overestimate by the pressure group of the amount of oil contained within the installation. Greenpeace estimated that the figure was 5,000 tonnes, while Shell had earlier given the figure of 30 tonnes (it should be emphasised, however, that because the measurements were made following the occupation, they played no part in Greenpeace's initial decision to take direct action). This highly embarrassing admission was made public on the first day of the Off-Shore Europe 95 conference, held in Aberdeen, 5–8 September, at which the Chairman of Shell UK, Dr C. E. Fay, was to be the opening, keynote speaker.

The last act of the Brent Spar saga began in November 1998 when Shell began to dismantle it in a Norwegian fjord. In July, the oil-exploring countries of the North Sea and North Atlantic, including Britain, had agreed that all oil platforms in the sea would be brought ashore for disposal, except the largest. It was estimated that Britain's agreement would cost the British oil industry £9 billion.

Source: Dickson, L. and McCulloch, A. 1996/1 'Shell, the Brent Spar and Greenpeace: a doomed tryst', in *Environmental Politics*, pp 397–410.

APPENDIX 8   THE ANTI-POLL TAX MOVEMENT

The anti-poll tax movement was at its most enthusiastic in February and March 1990 when it sprung into action with lobbying MPs, petitions etc. This fervent activity was too late, however: the legislation was in place and town-hall computers were preparing millions of bills.

Councils were called on to refuse to implement the tax. Again, the efforts were in vain. Only in the heartlands of municipal socialism were significant groups of councillors interested in defence of the law. Others were keen to obey Parliament, even if with a heavy heart.

High hopes were placed on the campaign of non-payment. This tapped into a long-time tradition of civil disobedience going back deep into British history. It had the rare advantage of combining strong moral anger with material self-interest.

The technical problems of the tax were immense with a mobile population, made worse by the fact that far more bills were issued than under the rating system. Every non-payer had to be taken to court and be given a hearing. The courts soon found ways to process large numbers of orders at once. They could make out hundreds and even a thousand or more liability orders in a day.

The problem for the authorities was not the action of getting the liability orders from the courts but getting cash from people who had had orders made against them. In practice, this was immensely difficult. The council could opt for deduction from salary or benefit; for the bailiffs to take property; or ultimately for jail for wilful non-payment. Deductions seemed like the easy way forward. They were already used for maintenance payments and fines. However, the sheer numbers involved largely defeated the councils. A large number of the councils which tried found that despite the threat of fines, very few people completed the forms. For example, in Exeter, only about 3 per cent did.

On the whole, bailiffs were not effective. This was because there were not many of them; they had not been geared up to the new demands put on them; their legal rights were very restricted, and anti-poll tax unions across Britain issued publicity advising how to thwart them; and finally, a bailiff's visit could be a lively confrontation between the local anti-poll tax protestors and the debt collector, with the protestors often winning.

A natural response from some of the more conservative councillors, of any party, was to jail non-payers. This raised the political profile, but it was a threat that was rarely used. The profile might be high, but it was not necessarily favourable.

The anti-poll tax movement was successful because it mobilised large numbers and found parts of the political system it could undermine.

Source: Barr, G. (1992) 'The anti-poll tax movement', in *Talking Politics*, The Politics Association, Vol. 4, No. 3, pp. 143–7.

GLOSSARY

Capitol   The building that houses Congress in the USA. Also, comparable buildings in the State capitals.

Cause group   A type of pressure group which seeks to act in the interests of a cause.

Constituency plan agreements   Agreements between trade unions and selected constituency Labour parties, involving some union money going to support constituency activities, in return for which the union has some representation on the general committee of the Constituency Labour Party.

Core executive   A complex web of institutions, networks and practices surrounding the Prime Minister, Cabinet, Cabinet committees and their official counterparts, less formalised ministerial 'clubs' or meetings, bilateral negotiations, and interdepartmental committees.

Corporatism   The concept of a system of pressure-group representation in which the constituent units are organised into a limited number of singular, compulsory, non-competitive, hierarchically ordered and functionally differentiated categories, recognised or licensed (if not created) by the State and granted a deliberate representational monopoly within their respective categories in exchange for observing certain controls on their selection of leaders and articulation of demands and supports.

Elitism   The theory that political power is concentrated in the hands of a few, the elite.

Insider group   A type of pressure group which is regarded as legitimate by government and is consulted on a regular basis.

Iron law of oligarchy   The theory that it is in the nature of organisations for power to be concentrated in the hands of a small group of dominant figures.

Issue network   A type of policy network which involves loose relationships between pressure groups and government.

Liberal corporatism   A type of corporatism under which the emphasis is on the relationships between government and a wide range of functional groups, or at least between government and all organisations that represent capital and labour.

Lobbying   Seeking to influence public policy-makers. The term originates in New York State politics when people eager to extract favours from legislators waited for them in the lobby of the State Capitol.

New Social Movements   Movements which emphasise lack of hierarchy and formal organisation.

Outsider group   A type of pressure group which either does not wish to become involved in regular discussion with officials, or would like to gain recognition by government but is unable to do so.

Pluralism   The concept of a system of pressure-group representation in which the constituent units are organised into an unspecified number of multiple, voluntary, competitive, non-hierarchically ordered and self-determined (as to type or scope of interest) categories which are not specially licensed, recognised, subsidised, created or otherwise controlled in leadership selection or interest articulation by the State, and which do not exercise a monopoly of representational activity within their respective categories.

Policy community   A type of policy network which involves close relationships between pressure groups and government.

Policy network   The concept which stresses that relationships between pressure groups and government vary between policy areas.

Post-materialism   The theory that as a growing proportion of the public begins to emphasise post-material values, the composition of the political agenda shifts from traditional economic and security concerns to the non-economic and quality-of-life values of a post-industrial society.

Pressure group   An organisation which seeks to influence a comparatively small range of public policy without itself seeking to govern.

Professional lobbyist   Someone who is professionally employed to lobby on behalf of clients, or who advises clients on how to lobby on their own behalf.

Promotional group   (see **cause group**).

Protest businesses   The argument that modern large-scale cause groups are the product of mail-order marketing.

Sectional group   A type of pressure group which looks after the common interests of a section of the community.

Single market   The free movement of goods, services, capital and labour within the EU.

Societal corporatism   A type of corporatism under which the corporations are autonomous but cooperate with the State and each other because they recognise that they are mutually interdependent.

Spokesperson group   (see **sectional group**)

State corporatism   A type of corporatism under which the State directs the corporations, which are subordinate to and dependent on the State.

Tripartism   A sub-type of liberal corporatism which emphasises the relationship between government and the peak organisations.

Westminster   The location of the Houses of Parliament.

Whitehall   The location of major government departments.

FURTHER READING AND RESOURCES

BOOKS

Ainley, P. and Vickerstaff, S. (1993) 'Translations from corporatism: the privatisation of policy failure', *Contemporary Record*, Vol. 7, No. 3, pp 541–56, London: Frank Cass.

Bachrach, P. and Baratz, M. (1962) 'Two faces of power', *American Political Science Review*, Vol. 56, pp 947–52, reprinted in Castles, F. G., Murray, D. J. and Potter D. C. (eds) (1971) *Decisions, Organizations and Society*, Harmondsworth: Penguin.

Baggot, R. (1992) 'The measurement of change in pressure group politics', *Talking Politics*, Vol. 5, No. 1, pp 18–22, Manchester: The Politics Association.

Baggot, R. (1995) *Pressure Groups Today*, Manchester: Manchester University Press.

Baldwin, M. (1990) 'The House of Lords', in Rush, M. (ed) *Parliament and Pressure Politics*, Oxford: Clarendon Press.

Bazalgette, P. (1996) 'When pressure groups get it wrong', in *Pressure Group Politics in Modern Britain*, London: The Social Market Foundation.

Beer, S. H. (1965) *Modern British Politics*, London: Faber and Faber.

Bennie, L. G. (1998) 'Brent Spar, Atlantic Oil and Greenpeace', *Parliamentary Affairs*, Vol. 51, No. 3, pp 397–410, Oxford: Oxford University Press.

Bentley, A. F. (1908) *The Process of Government*, Harvard: Harvard University Press.

Berry, S. (1992a) 'Lobbying – a need to regulate?' *Politics Review*, Vol. 2, No. 3, pp 23–6, Deddington: Philip Allan.

Berry, S. (1992b) 'Lobbyists: techniques of the political "insider"', *Parliamentary Affairs*, Vol. 45, No. 2, pp 220–32, Oxford: Oxford University Press.

Brenton, T. (1994) *The Greening of Machiavelli*, London: Earthscan.

Brittan, S. (1975) 'The economic contradictions of democracy', *British Journal of Political Science*, Vol. 5; shortened version in King, A. (ed) (1976) *Why is Britain becoming harder to govern?*, London: British Broadcasting Corporation.

Browne, W. P. (1990) 'Organized interests and their interest niches: a search for pluralism in a policy domain', *Journal of Politics*, Vol. 52, No. 2, pp 477–509.

Butler, D. and Kavanagh, D. (1997) *The British General Election of 1997*, Basingstoke: Macmillan.

Cigler, A. and Loomis, B. (eds) (1986) *Interest Group Politics*, Washington D.C.: Congressional Quarterly Press.

Cigler, A. and Loomis, B. (1995) 'Contemporary interest group politics: more than "more of the same"', in Cigler, A. and Loomis, B. (eds) *Interest Group Politics*, 4th edn, Washington D.C.: Congressional Quarterly Press.

Davies, Alan, (1998) *British Politics and Europe*, London: Hodder & Stoughton.

Doig, A. (1986) 'Access to Parliament and the rise of the professional lobbyist', *Public Money*, Vol. 5, No. 4, pp 39–43.

Dowse, R. E. and Hughes, J. A. (1977) 'Sporadic interventionists', *Political Studies*, Vol. 25, No. 1, pp 84–92.

Dunleavy, P. and Rhodes, R. A. W. (1990) 'Core executive studies in Britain', *Public Administration*, Vol. 68, No. 1, pp 3–28, Oxford: Basil Blackwell.

Eckstein, H. (1960) *Pressure Group Politics: The Case of the BMA*, London: Allen and Unwin.

Garner, R. (1993) *Animals, Politics and Morality*, Manchester: Manchester University Press.

Graham, D. and Tytler, D. (1993) *A Lesson For Us All*, London: Routledge and Kegan Paul.

Grant, W. (1990) 'Insider and outsider pressure groups', *Social Studies Review*, January 1990, Deddington: Philip Allan.

Grant, W. (1993a) 'Pressure groups', *Development in Politics*, Vol. 4, pp 57–77, Ormskirk: Causeway Press.

Grant, W. (1993b) *Business and Politics in Britain*, 2nd edn, London: Macmillan.

Grant, W. (1995a) *Pressure Groups, Politics and Democracy in Britain*, Hemel Hempstead: Harvester Wheatsheaf.

Grant, W. (1995b) 'Are environmental pressure groups effective?', *Politics Review*, Vol. 5, No. 1, pp 31–3, Deddington: Philip Allan.

Grant, W. (1996) 'Pressure groups', *Developments in Politics*, Vol. 7, pp 23–39, Ormskirk: Causeway Press.

Grant, W. and Marsh, D. (1977) *The CBI*, London: Hodder & Stoughton.

Gyford, (1986) *Research Volume IV: Aspects of Local Democracy*, *The Conduct of Local Authority Business*, London: HMSO *Cmnd 9801*.

Heclo, H. and Wildavsky, A. (1974) *The Private Government of Public Money*, London: Macmillan.

Inglehart, R. (1995) 'Public support for environmental protection: objective problems and subjective values in 43 societies, *PS: Political Science and Politics*, pp 57–72.

Jones, J. B. (1990) 'Party committees and all-party groups', in Rush, M. (ed) *Parliament and Pressure Politics*, Oxford: Clarendon Press.

Jordan, G. (1989) 'Insider lobbying: the British version', *Political Studies*, Vol. 37, No. 1, pp 107–13.

Jordan, G. and Maloney, W. (1997) *The Protest Business?* Manchester: Manchester University Press.

Jordan, G. Maloney, W. and McLaughlin, A. (1992) 'Insiders, outsiders and political access', in *British Interest Group Project, Working Paper Series No. 3*, Aberdeen: British Interest Group Project, University of Aberdeen.

Lehmbruch, G. (1974) 'Consociational democracy, class conflict and the new corporatism', paper presented to the IPSA Round Table on Political Integration, Jerusalem, pp 1–2.

Lowe, P. and Goyder, J. (1983) *Environmental Groups in Politics*, London: Allen and Unwin.

Lukes, S. (1975) *Power*, London: Macmillan.

McKenzie, R. T. (1958) 'Parties, pressure groups, and the British political process', *Political Quarterly*, Vol. 27, No. 1, pp 5–16, reprinted in Rose, R. (ed) (1967), *Studies in British Politics*, London: Macmillan.

Maloney, W., Jordan, G. and McLaughlin, A. (1992) 'The insider/outsider model revisited', *Journal of Public Policy*, Vol. 14, No. 1, pp 17–38.

Marsh, D. (ed) (1983) *Pressure groups: interest groups in Britain*, London: Junction Books.

Marsh, D. and Read, M. (1988) *Private Members Bills*, Cambridge: Cambridge University Press.

Marsh, D. and Rhodes, R. (eds) (1992) *Policy Networks in British Government*, Oxford: Clarendon Press.

Maslow, A. H. (1943) 'A theory of human motivation', in Shafritz, J. M. and Hyde, A. C. (eds) *Classics of Public Administration*, 3rd edn, California: Brooks/Cole.

May, T. and Nugent, N. (1982) 'Insiders, outsiders and thresholders', paper presented to the Conference of Political Studies Association, University of Kent.

Mazey, S. and Richardson, J. (1993) 'Pressure groups and the EC', *Politics Review*, Vol. 3, No. 1, pp 20–4, Deddington: Philip Allan.

McNaughton, N. (1999) *The Prime Minister and Cabinet Government*, London: Hodder & Stoughton.

Michels, R. (1911) *Political Parties: A Sociological Study of the Oligarchical Tendencies of Modern Democracy*, New York: Collier.

Miller, C. (1990) *Lobbying Government*, Oxford: Basil Blackwell.

Mitchell, N. J. (1987) 'Changing pressure group politics: the case of the Trades Union Congress, 1976–84', *British Journal of Political Science*, Vol. 17, No. 4, pp 509–17.

Neill Committee (1998) *Fifth Report of the Committee on Standards in Public Life, Cmnd 4507*, London: HMSO.

Newton, K. (1976) *Second City Politics*, Oxford: Oxford University Press.

Nolan Committee (1995) *First Report of the Committee on Standards in Public Life, Cmnd 2850*, London: HMSO.

Norton, P. (1990) 'Public legislation', in Rush, M. *Parliament and Pressure Politics*, Oxford: Clarendon Press.

Olson, M. (1965) *The Logic of Collective Action*, Harvard University Press, excerpts reprinted in Castles, F. G., Murray, D. J. and Potter D. C. (eds) (1971) *Decisions, Organizations and Society*, Harmondsworth: Penguin.

Parry, G., Moyser, G. and Day, N. (1992) *Political Participation and Democracy in Britain*, Cambridge: Cambridge University Press.

Potter, A. (1961) *Organized Groups in British National Politics*, London: Faber and Faber.

Poulantzas, N. (1975) *Classes in Contemporary Capitalism*, London: New Left Books.

Richardson, J. J. (1993) 'Interest group behaviour in Britain: continuity and change', in Richardson, J. (ed) *Pressure Groups*, Oxford: Oxford University Press.

Richardson, J. J. and Jordan, G. (1979) *Governing Under Pressure*, Oxford: Martin Robertson.

Richardson, J., Maloney, W. and Rudig, W. (1992) 'The dynamics of policy change: lobbying and water privatisation', *Public Administration*, Vol. 70, No. 2, pp 157–75, Oxford: Basil Blackwell.

Riddell, P. (1996) 'Pressure groups, media and government', in *Pressure Group Politics in Modern Britain*, London: The Social Market Foundation.

Rucht, D. (1993) '"Think globally, act locally?" Needs, forms and problems of cross-national cooperation among environmental groups', in Liefferink, J. D., Lowe, P. and Mol, A. P. J. (eds) *European Integration and Environmental Policy*, London: Belhaven.

Rush, M. (ed) (1990a) *Parliament and Pressure Politics*, Oxford: Clarendon Press.

Rush, M. (1990b) 'Lobbying Parliament', *Parliamentary Affairs*, Vol. 43, No. 2, pp 141–8, Oxford: Oxford University Press.

Rush, M. (1990c) 'Select committees', in Rush, M. (ed) *Parliament and Pressure Politics*, Oxford: Clarendon Press.

Sargent, J. A. (1993) 'The corporate benefits of lobbying: the British case and its relevance to the European Community', in Mazey, S. and Richardson, J. (eds) *Lobbying in the European Community*, Oxford: Oxford University Press.

Schattschneider, E. E. (1960) *The Semisovereign People*, New York: Holt, Rinehart and Winston.

Schmitter, P. (1974) 'Still the century of corporatism?', *Review of Politics*, Vol. 36, pp 85–131; and in Schmitter, P. and Lehmbruch, G. (eds) (1979), *Trends Towards Corporatist Intermediation*, London: Sage.

Self, P. and Storing, H. J. (1962) *The State and the Farmer*, London: Allen and Unwin.

Seyd, P. and Whitely, P. (1992) *Labour's Grass Roots: The Politics of Party Membership*, Oxford: Clarendon Press.

Simpson, D. (1998) *UK Government and Politics*, London: Hodder & Stoughton.

Smith, M. J. (1992) 'The agricultural policy community: the rise and fall of a closed relationship', in Marsh, D. and Rhodes, R. (eds) *Policy Networks in British Government*, Oxford: Clarendon Press.

Stewart, J. D. (1958) *British Pressure Groups*, Oxford: Oxford University Press.

Stoker, G. (1991) *The Politics of Local Government*, 2nd edn, London: Macmillan.

Toke, D. (1996) 'Power and environmental pressure groups', *Talking Politics*, Vol. 9, No. 2, pp 107–15, Manchester: The Politics Association.

Truman, D. (1951) *The Governmental Process*, New York: Knopf.

Waldegrave, W. (1996) 'Politicians and pressure groups', in *Pressure Group Politics in Modern Britain*, London: The Social Market Foundation.

Watts, D. (1993) 'Lobbying Europe', in *Talking Politics*, Vol. 5, No. 2, Manchester: The Politics Association.

Whitely, P. and Winyard, S. (1987) *Pressure for the Poor*, London: Methuen.

Wilson, D. (1984) *Pressure: The A to Z of Campaigning in Britain*, London: Heinemann; adaptation (1988) 'In defence of pressure groups' in *Contemporary Record*, Vol. 2, No. 1, p 15, Deddington: Philip Allan.

JOURNALS

Relevant articles appear in the following journals:

Talking Politics, the Journal of the Politics Association, Old Hall Lane, Manchester M13 0XT.

Politics Review, Philip Allan Publishers, Market Place, Deddington, Oxfordshire OX15 0SE.

Developments in Politics, Causeway Press Ltd., PO Box 13, Ormskirk, Lancashire L39 5HP.

Parliamentary Affairs, Oxford University Press, Great Clarendon Street, Oxford OX2 6DP, in association with the Hansard Society for Parliamentary Government, St. Philips Building North, Sheffield St, London WC2A 2EX. The 1998 special issue, vol. 51, No. 3, protest politics: cause groups and campaigns.

CONFERENCES

One-day conferences are currently organised by, for example:

Enterprise Education Conferences, 4 Princess Road, London NW1 8JJ. Tel.: 0171 483 1349.

Student Educational Conferences, Weavers Lodge, The Green, Stalham, NR12 9QA. Tel.: 01692 582565/582770.

The Politics Association (see previous address). Tel.: 0161 256 3906.

Easter Revision Conferences are also provided by Student Educational Conferences and the Politics Association in London and Manchester.

EXAMINING BOARDS' PUBLICATIONS

Syllabuses, Specimen Papers and Marking Schemes, Syllabus Support Material, Question Papers, Marking Schemes and Chief Examiners' Reports.

INDEX

Numbers in **bold** refer to pages on which there is a definition in the glossary.

ACCESS TO POLITICS

Access to Politics is a series of concise and readable topic books for politics students. Each book provides advice on note-taking, tackling exam questions, developing skills of analysis, evaluation and presentation, and reading around the subject.

TITLES PUBLISHED IN 1998:

TITLES PUBLISHING IN 1999:

See page iv for information on how to order copies.